THE COMPLETE INSTANT POT KETOGENIC MEAL PREP COOKBOOK

Kyle Moore

CONTENTS

INTRODUCTION

How to become healthy and fit? How to live a long and happy life? There is a secret to eating well, without investing in an expensive cookware or spending all your money on takeout. It is meal prepping! In addition, you should find a well-balanced diet for life-long health. Finally yet importantly, you should find good recipes so you can start your own culinary journey.

If you're new to meal prepping and wondering where to start, this cookbook may provide the answers. We will introduce you to the magical world of meal prepping so you can create your own culinary masterpieces in the future. You will be able to save more time in the kitchen and eat healthier. Cooking at home and meal prepping bring a family together. Whether you tend to cook something simple for Sunday breakfast or a special holiday dinner, you are sure to love this recipe collection. You will learn to make traditional recipes such as hearty soups and stews as well as innovative recipes such as vegan Mushroom Stroganoff or Brownie Squares with Blackberry-Goat Cheese Swirl. This is a huge inspiration, so let's get it on!

BENEFITS OF MEAL PREPPING

Health benefits: You are what you eat.

Eating is not just about satisfying the appetite. Food affects our health, our social life and general well-being. At the very least, food is our source of energy so it affects our productivity. Common processed foods may be linked to poor mental health and many modern diseases, many researchers suggest. Further, the risk of cancer, in particular, is associated with greater consumption of junk food.

A healthy eating plan includes consuming a well-balanced diet rich in plants and seafood and eliminating processed foods, sugars and additives. Many studies have found that cooking at home can help you maintain your physical and mental health. It can be especially beneficial if you have a food allergy or other health issue. Family dinners are an extremely important part of a healthy lifestyle; when families eat together, they are much healthier. In addition, you can involve your kids in food preparation and meal prepping, which is a smart way to teach them good habits.

It is well known that good eating habits are linked to a healthy lifestyle. Commit to becoming healthy today, and remember – "Think positively and exercise daily, eat healthy, work hard, stay strong, build faith, worry less, read more, and be happy." Anonymous

A massive time saver.

One of the best parts of meal prep is an ability to plan your day and week. This is one of the best time-saving strategies in the kitchen. Cooking at home is easier than you could have ever imagined; in addition, it is faster and less expensive than dining out.

By planning your meals in advance and having a good amount of staples in your freezer, eating a healthy diet will become second nature. Most recipes in this cookbook are focused on fast prep times around 30 minutes. You can choose only one recipe to start with, so it can be made for lunch today and reheated for dinner tomorrow. Just choose the recipe that matches all your requirements. On the other hand, you can cook a larger amount of food (double or triple the recipe) over the weekend, portion it all out, and enjoy favorite dish all week long. This is one of the easiest ways to fit cooking into your already busy schedules and feed the whole family. Meal prepping is not just about feeding your body; it's about feeling that you are doing something right; in fact, meal prepping gives you a peace of mind!

A great way to save money in your day-to-day life.

If you're into large-batch cooking, you can save a lot of money. You should choose freezer-friendly recipes that call for affordable ingredients. Further, you can repurpose different foods for multiple meals. You can also utilize leftovers. Keep it simple and do not fall into the trap to buy 10 different types of vegetables; you won't use all of them and all they will go bad soon. For instance, you can find green beans on sale or buy them in bulk; then, you can cook them, freeze them in storage containers, and use for salads, soups, or stews.

It can help you maintain a healthy weight.

Needless to say, when you are planning meals in advance, you have a total control over your eating. Portion control is an extremely important component of a well-thought out diet.

This is a great way to balance your diet, calculate calories and macronutrients and keep up your personal fitness. First things first, answer a simple question: What is favorable for your body? Home-cooked meals that are chock full of fresh, whole ingredients or commercially prepared foods that are high in sugar and trans fats? Throw out junk food because when "bad" foods are not in your kitchen, then you can't eat them, can't you! Less cheating, more discipline! Undoubtedly, meal prepping is one of the best ways to stay healthy and happy in your own skin!

FIVE SECRETS OF PEOPLE WHO MEAL PREP

Busy people (ordinary people like you and me) with healthy eating habits are willing to share with you a foolproof method for effective, achievable and easy meal prep and planning. Below, we have outlined the basics, providing some handy tips and tricks.

1) Plan your weekly menu. How many meals do you need? The first thing to do to avoid wasting food is to calculate how many dinners, lunches, breakfast, desserts or snacks you really need throughout the week. Make a shopping list and keep it in order.

2) Keep it simple. Take shortcuts and choose simple meals that everyone loves. Avoid experimenting, especially at the very beginning. Forget trends and just make real food for you and your family. Make chili or pulled pork for lunch. Make omelet for breakfast or stick to the same dinner every night (for instance, variations of grilled fish fillets and fresh salads). Your goal is to keep your body healthy and well fed, and it's not rocket science!

3) Be prepared. Keep your kitchen stocked with quick go-to ingredients such as frozen veggies, chicken fillets, tomato sauce and good chicken stock. Do your mis en place – cut up fruits and veggies in advance and you will have the best ingredients of the season. Make the most of your weekend and get your meal prepping done on Sunday afternoon. Moreover, you can set a timer and you'll be amazed at how this trick improves your organization skills and eating habits. Be prepared and you will never make poor nutrition decisions!

4) Multitasking is not necessarily bad. When it comes to meal prepping, multitasking is your friend. However, there are a few major points to keep in mind. Read the recipe thoroughly before you turn the stove on. Roast two large-sized trays of vegetables at a time. Clean your work surface and dishes as you go. If your recipe calls for 10 minutes of simmering, use that time to chop other ingredients, clean up a mess, or set the table. Cooking does not have to be boring. You can listen to audio books or language courses.

5) Use the right tool for the job. It is a common-sense advice and that is so true. Consider buying an electric pressure cooker to speed up your cooking. Invest in good storage containers, a good-quality cutting board, and blender. Utilize technology and find meal-planning apps on the Internet (many of them are totally free).

BASIC KETO RULES

How does a keto diet works? A ketogenic diet is a dietary regimen in which you choose low-carb, high-fat and high-protein foods. When you eat food that is high in carbs, your body produces glucose and uses it as a primary energy source. Since your body burns the glucose, the fats for foods are actually stored in your cells. Therefore, you cannot lose weight. On the other hand, during a low-carb diet your body makes *ketones*; then, your body burns ketones as the primary fuel source. This process is called *ketosis*; in other words, this metabolic state occurs when the body starts producing ketones.

Putting the body into a state of ketosis is your main goal on a keto diet. You can do that by reducing a daily calorie intake or your intake of carbohydrates. Researchers suggest that reducing carbohydrate intake by 40 grams per day can ensure safe weight loss over a long period of time. You can achieve your diet goals by following these guidelines: 5-10% of calories should come from carbohydrates; 20-25% of calories should come from protein; 70-80% of calories should come from fat.

There are a few clear signs that you are in the state of ketosis: dry mouth syndrome and bad breath, short-term fatigue, a frequent need to go to urinate, a noticeable increase in energy, decrease in hunger, weight loss, and so on. If you're not sure, you can use a blood ketone meter, urine sticks or breath ketone meters.

Foods recommended on a keto diet include:

- **Non-starchy vegetables that grow above ground** – celery, cauliflower, broccoli, greens cabbage, peppers, tomato, green beans, mushrooms, asparagus, Brussels sprouts, onions, leeks.

- **Poultry and Red Meats** (preferably grass-fed) – pork, beef, goat, veal, chicken, turkey, and duck.

- **Fish & Shellfish** (preferably wild-caught) – salmon, cod, haddock, tuna, tilapia, and prawns.

- **Eggs and Dairy products** – whole milk, heavy cream, full-fat cheese, unsweetened yogurt, butter, and ghee.

- **Nuts and seeds**

- **Fruits** – berries and avocado.

- **Fats & Oils** – olive oil, coconut oil, nut butter, canola oil, flaxseed oil, MCT (medium chain triglycerides) oil, lard, and tallow.

- **Sweeteners** – monk fruit powder, xylitol, erythritol, stevia, yacon sweetener, and Splenda.

- **Condiments** (make sure to check the ingredients carefully) – most tomato sauces, soy sauce, most hot sauces, coconut aminos, pickles, Caesar and ranch dressing, Alfredo sauce, fermented foods, mustard, vinegar, mayonnaise, and homemade sauces.

- **Fermented soy products**

- **Spices and herbs**

- **Beverages** – coffee, tea, unsweetened lemonade, sparkling water, seltzer, low-carb smoothies, and diet soda.

- **Alcoholic beverages** – hard liquor, unsweetened wines, champagne, spirits (for instance, whiskey, brandy and dry martini contain zero carbs), and light beer.

Foods that are strictly off-limits include grains, sugar, dry beans, cereals, grain flour, starchy fruits such as bananas, and root vegetables. The main foods to stay away from to achieve all the benefits of the keto diet are processed foods that contain carbohydrates.

A KETO DIET: KEEP IT SIMPLE

Do not overthink your diet.

Although a diet plan might seem overwhelming, it's not that complicated. First things first, simply stop eating packaged food and consume whole, organic food. Insist on real, nutrition-dense foods and you'll be on the right track. Do not worry too much, relax, and try to eat unprocessed foods.

Make things easier and faster.

A keto diet can help you start losing weight fast, transforming your body into a fat-burning machine! To make things easier, start your day with a high-protein breakfast. It will eliminate sugar cravings and reduce daily calorie intake. It is not about eating less, it's about eating more real foods.

Drink water.

How much water should we drink per day? Experts recommend eight to ten 8-ounce glasses of water per day. Drinking water can increase ketosis so you will burn more fats and stay hydrated at the same time. Recent studies have proven that drinking water a half hour before a meal can speed up our metabolism and increase weight loss by 44%!

Spice it up!

If you like a spicy food, we have good news for you – Spicy food can boost your metabolism! For instance, capsaicin, an important component of chili peppers, will fire up your metabolism. Add chili peppers, hot sauce or black pepper to your meal and you will increase your metabolism by as much as 20%.

Eat high-protein foods. They can help you lose weight naturally.

The recent study in the American Journal of Clinical Nutrition Plus has found out that protein can increase your metabolism and boost post-meal calorie burn by 35 %.You can eat eggs and full-fat dairy products for breakfast to jumpstart your metabolism in the morning. It can help you reduce your appetite significantly, cuts cravings, and prevent muscle loss. For lunch, pile your plate with non-starchy vegetables and protein. Eat a protein-packed soup for dinner. You can find a long list of great high-protein foods on a keto food list so go for it!

A few secrets of skinny people.

Choose foods with high water content such as soups and fresh salads. Drink cold water to speed up your metabolism naturally. Drink a cup of green tea per day. Fill your plate with mostly vegetables and lean protein such as chicken breasts or white fish. Opt for foods that are slow to digest (for instance, make scrambled eggs with a teaspoon of olive oil and a handful of mixed peppers; garnish with a tablespoon of seeds).

It may sound unrealistic but skinny people don't skip meals (especially breakfast) because they tend to avoid overeating for the next meal. Further, every thin person strives to find the perfect diet for his/her body type and health goals. These people do not feel like they are dieting, a certain dietary regimen simply becomes their way of life. And last but not least – they exercise regularly. The more you learn about ketogenic lifestyle, the easier it gets! Maybe, it's going to be hard. Really. However, it is not impossible.

21-DAY KETOGENIC MEAL PLAN

To put it into perspective, we created an easy-to-follow meal plan for 21 days. Ready, steady, go!

DAY 1

Breakfast – Breakfast Meatloaf Cups

Lunch – Winter Beef Soup; 2 slices of cheese; 1 handful of iceberg lettuce

Dinner – Malabar Fish Curry

DAY 2

Breakfast – 2 hard-boiled eggs; 1 slice of cheese; 1 slice of bacon

Lunch – Favorite Beef Paprikash; 1 serving of cauliflower rice; 1 large handful of lettuce

Dinner – Winter Chicken Salad

DAY 3

Breakfast – Scamorza Open Tart

Lunch – The Best Ever Chicken Goulash; 1 medium tomato

Dinner – Chicken Liver Pâté; 1 keto dinner roll; 1 cup raw baby spinach with apple cider vinegar

DAY 4

Breakfast – Omelet with veggies; 1 slice of hard cheese

Lunch – Gruyère and Turkey Au Gratin; 1 serving of coleslaw

Dinner – Turnip Greens with Sausage; 1 medium tomato

DAY 5

Breakfast – Mini Meatloaves with Cheese; a dollop of sour cream; 1-2 pickles

Lunch – Beef Stew with a Twist; 1 handful of fresh arugula salad with 1 teaspoon of mustard and a few drizzles of a freshly squeezed lemon juice

Dinner – Zucchini Keto Lasagna

DAY 6

Breakfast – Skillet-Baked Eggs with Spinach; 1 slice of keto bread

Lunch – Winter One-Pot-Wonder; 1 serving of cauliflower rice; Greek-style salad (tomato, cucumber, bell peppers, feta cheese)

Dinner – Za'atar-Rubbed Pork Shank; 1 serving of low-carb grilled vegetables

DAY 7

Breakfast – Rum Coconut Granola; 1/2 cup of almond milk

Lunch – Pork Cutlets with Porcini Mushroom Sauce; 1 large tomato

Dinner – Thai Coconut Chicken; 1 serving of cauliflower rice

DAY 8

Breakfast – Indian Egg Muffins; 1/2 cup of Greek-style yogurt

Lunch – The Best Pork Chile Verde; 1 serving of coleslaw

Dinner – Basil Wine Scallops; 1 green bell pepper; 1 garlic clove

DAY 9

Breakfast – Scrambled eggs; 1 slice of bacon; 1 tomato

Lunch – Hot Spicy Chicken Soup; 1 serving of cabbage salad

Dinner – Chicken Wings Italiano

DAY 10

Breakfast – Cauliflower Breakfast Cups; 1/2 cup of almond milk

Lunch – Creamy Turkey Breasts with Mushrooms; 1 green bell pepper; 1 scallion

Dinner – Kid-Friendly Mini Frittatas; a dollop of sour cream

DAY 11

Breakfast – 1 tablespoon of peanut butter; 1 slice of keto bread

Lunch – Chicken Parm Chowder; 1 serving of low-carb grilled vegetables

Dinner – Beef Short Ribs with Cilantro Cream

DAY 12

Breakfast – Sunday Sweet Porridge; 1/2 cup of almond milk

Lunch – Chicken Legs in Mustard Curry Sauce; 1 serving of cabbage salad

Dinner – Italian-Style Turkey Meatloaf; 1 serving of roasted bell peppers

DAY 13

Breakfast – Cheesy Cauliflower Balls

Lunch – Beef Medley with Sausage; 1 medium cucumber; 1 scallion

Dinner – Chili Hot Dog Bake

DAY 14

Breakfast – Fluffy Berry Cupcakes

Lunch – Thick Flank Steak Chili; 1 medium tomato

Dinner – Simple Garlicky Halibut Steak; a handful of baby spinach with champagne vinegar

DAY 15

Breakfast – Winter Bacon and Leek Quiche

Lunch – Buffalo Thick Pork Soup; 1 serving of roasted keto veggies

Dinner – Bok Choy Boats with Shrimp Salad

DAY 16

Breakfast – Spinach and Cheese Muffins; 1/2 cup of Greek-style yogurt

Lunch – Cheesy Chicken and Mushroom Casserole

Dinner – Family Pork Roast; 1 large handful of lettuce with 1 teaspoon of mustard; Vanilla Rum Flan

DAY 17

Breakfast – 2 hard-boiled eggs; 2 slices of Cheddar cheese

Lunch – Vegan Mushroom Stroganoff; 1 slice of keto bread

Dinner – Hot Lager Chicken Wings

DAY 18

Breakfast – Asian-Style Savory Egg Custard

Lunch – Mediterranean Pork Cutlets; 1 serving of Greek salad

Dinner – Indian-Style Cauliflower

DAY 19

Breakfast – Special Breakfast Eggs; 1 cucumber

Lunch – Greek-Style Pork Stew; 1 serving of steamed broccoli

Dinner – Herbed Cod Steaks; 1 serving of steamed kale

DAY 20

Breakfast – Hangover Seafood Bowl

Lunch – Ground Pork Taco Bowl; 1 large handful of iceberg lettuce

Dinner – Vegetables à la Grecque

DAY 21

Breakfast – Zingy Habanero Eggs; 1 serving of blue cheese

Lunch – The Best Fish Chili; 1 serving of roasted eggplant

Dinner – 1 steamed chicken breast; 1 serving of roasted asparagus; Grandma's Orange Cheesecake

COOKED FOODS

Recommended Storage Times

FOOD	MONTHS	FOOD	MONTHS
Cooked meat	2-3	Pasta, cooked	3
Ham, cooked	2	Rice, cooked	3
Meat dishes	2-3	Baked bread & Rolls	2-3
Gravy & Meat broth	2-3	Baked cake	2-3
Fried chicken	4	Baked fruit pieces	6-8
Poultry, pieces covered with broth or gravy	6	Cheesecake	2-3
Chicken nuggets, patties	1-3	Baked muffins	6-12
Cooked poultry dishes	4-6	Pancakes	3
Meat soups & stews	2-3	Waffles	1
Ham, fully cooked, whole	1-2	Ice cream	2
Ham, fully cooked, slices	1-2		
Cooked fish	4-6		
Vegetable soups & stews	2-3		
Casserole, cooked	3		

BREAKFAST

1. Kale and Tomato Frittata

Servings 3

Ingredients

- 5 eggs, whisked
- 1 cup fresh kale leaves, torn into pieces
- 1 green bell pepper, seeded and chopped
- 1 jalapeño pepper, seeded and minced
- 1 fresh ripe tomato, chopped
- Sea salt and ground black pepper, to taste
- 1/2 teaspoon cayenne pepper
- 2 tablespoons scallions, chopped
- 1 garlic clove, minced

Directions

1. Spritz a baking pan that fits inside your Instant Pot with a nonstick cooking spray.
2. Thoroughly combine all the ingredients and spoon the mixture into the prepared baking pan. Cover with a sheet of foil.
3. Add 1 cup of water and a metal trivet to the Instant Pot. Lower the baking pan onto the trivet.
4. Secure the lid. Choose "Manual" mode and Low pressure; cook for 6 minutes. Once cooking is complete, use a natural pressure release; remove the lid carefully.
5. Let cool completely before storing.

Ready in about 10 minutes

NUTRITIONAL INFORMATION (Per Serving)

140 - Calories
7.3g - Fat
6.1g - Carbs
11.2g - Protein
2.8g - Sugars

Storing

- Cut the frittata into three wedges. Place each of them in an airtight container; place in the refrigerator for up 3 to 4 days.
- To freeze, place in separate Ziploc bags and freeze up to 3 months. To defrost, place in your microwave for a few minutes.

2. Scamorza Open Tart

Servings 4

Ready in about 30 minutes

NUTRITIONAL INFORMATION (Per Serving)

350 - Calories
25.1g - Fat
4.8g - Carbs
25.9g - Protein
2.9g - Sugars

Ingredients

- 5 eggs, beaten
- 1/3 cup double cream
- Salt and ground black pepper, to taste
- 1 teaspoon cayenne pepper
- 5 ounces speck, chopped
- 1/4 cup scallions, chopped
- 1/2 cup Scamorza cheese, crumbled
- 1 bunch of Rucola, to serve

Directions

1. Begin by adding 1 cup of water and a metal rack to your Instant Pot. Then, spritz a heatproof bowl and set aside.
2. In a mixing dish, thoroughly combine the eggs, cream, salt, black pepper, and cayenne pepper. Add the chopped speck, scallions, and cheese.
3. Spoon the mixture into the prepared heatproof bowl; cover with a piece of aluminum foil, making a foil sling.
4. Secure the lid. Choose "Manual" mode and High pressure; cook for 25 minutes. Once cooking is complete, use a quick pressure release; carefully remove the lid.

Storing

- Cut the tart into four pieces. Place the pieces in covered airtight containers to prevent drying out; keep in the refrigerator for 3 to 4 days.
- For freezing, place the pieces in heavy-duty freezer bags and freeze up to 4 months. Defrost in your microwave for a couple of minutes. Enjoy!

3. Indian Egg Muffins

Servings 5

Ready in about 10 minutes

NUTRITIONAL INFORMATION (Per Serving)

202 - Calories
13.7g - Fat
4.7g - Carbs
15.4g - Protein
2.6g - Sugars

Ingredients

- 5 eggs
- Seasoned salt and ground black pepper, to taste
- 2 green chilies, minced
- 5 tablespoons feta cheese, crumbled
- 1/2 tablespoon Chaat masala powder
- 1 tablespoon fresh cilantro, finely chopped

Directions

1. Begin by adding 1 cup of water and a steamer basket to your Instant Pot.
2. Mix all ingredients together; then, spoon the egg/cheese mixture into silicone muffin cups.
3. Next, lower your muffin cups onto the steamer basket.
4. Secure the lid. Choose "Manual" mode and High pressure; cook for 7 minutes. Once cooking is complete, use a quick pressure release; carefully remove the lid.
5. Let your muffins sit for a few minutes before removing from the cups.

Storing

- Place your muffins in airtight containers or Ziploc bags; keep in the refrigerator for a week.
- For freezing, divide the muffins among three Ziploc bags and freeze up to 3 months. Defrost in your microwave for a couple of minutes. Bon appétit!

4. Rum Coconut Granola

Servings 6

Ingredients

- 1 cup almonds
- 1 cup walnuts
- 2 ounces shredded coconut, unsweetened
- 1/4 cup sunflower seeds
- 1/4 cup pumpkin seeds
- 1 teaspoon vanilla paste
- 1/2 teaspoon ground cinnamon
- A pinch of kosher salt
- 1/4 teaspoon star anise, ground
- 2 tablespoons dark rum

**Ready in about
2 hours 35 minutes**

Directions

1. Place all ingredients in your Instant Pot.
2. Secure the lid. Choose "Slow Cook" mode and High pressure; cook for 2 hours 30 minutes. Once cooking is complete, use a quick pressure release; carefully remove the lid.
3. Spoon into individual bowls.

**NUTRITIONAL
INFORMATION
(Per Serving)**

166 - Calories
14.2g - Fat
4.4g - Carbs
4.8g - Protein
0.9g - Sugars

Storing

- The granola can be stored in airtight containers, in a cool, dry place for 3 months.
- For freezing, pack the granola into airtight freezer-safe containers. Gently press down on the granola to prevent freezer burn. Freeze for 3 months for the best quality.
- To thaw the frozen granola, let it come to room temperature.

5. Sunday Sweet Porridge

Servings 2

Ingredients

- 2 tablespoons flaxseed meal
- 4 tablespoons coconut flour
- 1 tablespoon pumpkin seeds, chopped
- 1 tablespoon raw almonds, ground
- 1 cup unsweetened almond milk
- 1 cup water
- 1/8 teaspoon Monk fruit powder

Ready in about 10 minutes

Directions

1. Add all ingredients to the Instant Pot.
2. Secure the lid. Choose "Manual" mode and High pressure; cook for 5 minutes. Once cooking is complete, use a quick pressure release; carefully remove the lid. Let cool completely before storing.

NUTRITIONAL INFORMATION (Per Serving)

308 - Calories
30.6g - Fat
5.9g - Carbs
5.6g - Protein
1.1g - Sugars

Storing

- Spoon your porridge into two airtight containers; keep in your refrigerator for up to 4 to 6 days.
- For freezing, place your porridge in airtight containers or heavy-duty freezer bags. It will maintain the best quality for about 6 months. Defrost in the refrigerator. Bon appétit!

6. Spinach and Cheese Muffins

Servings 6

Ready in about
15 minutes

**NUTRITIONAL
INFORMATION
(Per Serving)**

236 - Calories
18.8g - Fat
3.3g - Carbs
13.2g - Protein
2.2g - Sugars

Ingredients

- 6 eggs
- 1/3 cup double cream
- 1/4 cup cream cheese
- Sea salt and freshly ground black pepper, to taste
- 1/2 teaspoon cayenne pepper
- 1 ½ cups spinach, chopped
- 1/4 cup green onions, chopped
- 1 ripe tomato, chopped
- 1/2 cup cheddar cheese, grated

Directions

1. Start by adding 1 cup of water and a metal rack to the Instant Pot. Now, spritz a muffin tin with a nonstick cooking spray.
2. In a mixing dish, thoroughly combine the eggs, double cream, cream cheese, salt, black pepper, and cayenne pepper.
3. Then, divide the spinach, green onions, tomato, and scallions among the cups. Pour the egg mixture over the vegetables. Top with the cheddar cheese.
4. Lower the cups onto the rack.
5. Secure the lid. Choose "Manual" mode and High pressure; cook for 10 minutes. Once cooking is complete, use a natural pressure release; carefully remove the lid. Let cool completely before storing.

Storing

- Place your muffins in the airtight containers or Ziploc bags; keep in the refrigerator for a week.
- For freezing, divide the muffins among Ziploc bags and freeze up to 3 months. Defrost in your microwave for a couple of minutes. Bon appétit!

7. Breakfast Meatloaf Cups

Servings 8

Ingredients

- 1 pound ground pork
- 1 pound ground beef
- 1/2 cup onion, chopped
- 2 garlic cloves, minced
- Salt and ground black pepper, to taste
- 1/3 cup Romano cheese, grated
- 1/4 cup pork rinds, crushed
- 4 eggs, whisked
- 2 ripe tomatoes, puréed
- 1/4 cup barbecue sauce, sugar-free

Ready in about 40 minutes

Directions

1. Start by adding 1 cup of water and a metal trivet to the bottom of your Instant Pot.
2. In a mixing bowl, thoroughly combine the ground meat, onion, garlic, salt, black pepper, cheese, pork rinds, and eggs.
3. Mix until everything is well incorporated. Divide the mixture among muffin cups.
4. In a small mixing bowl, whisk the puréed tomatoes with barbecue sauce. Lastly, top your muffins with the tomato sauce.
5. Secure the lid. Choose "Manual" mode and High pressure; cook for 25 minutes. Once cooking is complete, use a quick pressure release; carefully remove the lid.
6. Allow them to cool for 10 minutes before removing from the muffin tin.

Storing

- Wrap the meatloaf cups tightly with heavy-duty aluminum foil or plastic wrap. Then, keep in your refrigerator for up to 3 to 4 days.
- For freezing, wrap the meatloaf cups tightly to prevent freezer burn. Freeze up to 3 to 4 months. Defrost in the refrigerator. Bon appétit!

NUTRITIONAL INFORMATION (Per Serving)

375 - Calories
22.2g - Fat
5.5g - Carbs
35.4g - Protein
4.5g - Sugars

8. Fluffy Berry Cupcakes

Servings 6

Ready in about
30 minutes

NUTRITIONAL
INFORMATION
(Per Serving)

238 - Calories
21.6g - Fat
4.1g - Carbs
7.5g - Protein
2.2g - Sugars

Ingredients

- 1/4 cup coconut oil, softened
- 3 ounces cream cheese, softened
- 1/4 cup double cream
- 4 eggs
- 1/4 cup coconut flour
- 1/4 cup almond flour
- A pinch of salt
- 1/3 cup Swerve, granulated
- 1 teaspoon baking powder
- 1/4 teaspoon cardamom powder
- 1/2 teaspoon star anise, ground
- 1/2 cup fresh mixed berries

Directions

1. Start by adding 1 ½ cups of water and a metal rack to your Instant Pot.
2. Mix the coconut oil, cream cheese, and double cream in a bowl. Fold in the eggs, one at a time, and continue to mix until everything is well incorporated.
3. In another bowl, thoroughly combine the flour, salt, Swerve, baking powder, cardamom, and anise.
4. Add the cream/egg mixture to this dry mixture. Afterwards, fold in the fresh berries and gently stir to combine.
5. Divide the batter between silicone cupcake liners. Cover with a piece of foil. Place the cupcakes on the rack.
6. Secure the lid. Choose "Manual" mode and High pressure; cook for 25 minutes. Once cooking is complete, use a natural pressure release; carefully remove the lid. Let cool completely.

Storing

- Refrigerate the cupcakes covered loosely with plastic wrap. Keep in your refrigerator for up to 7 days.
- To freeze, wrap the cupcakes tightly with foil or place in heavy-duty freezer bag; freeze for about 2 to 3 months. Bon appétit!

9. Cauliflower Breakfast Cups

Servings 6

Ready in about 15 minutes

NUTRITIONAL INFORMATION (Per Serving)

335 - Calories
25.9g - Fat
5.8g - Carbs
19.8g - Protein
2.6g - Sugars

Ingredients

- 1/2 pound cauliflower, riced
- Sea salt and ground black pepper, to taste
- 1/2 teaspoon cayenne pepper
- 1/2 teaspoon dried dill weed
- 1/2 teaspoon dried basil
- 1/4 teaspoon dried oregano
- 2 tablespoons olive oil
- 2 garlic cloves, minced
- 1/2 cup scallions, chopped
- 1 cup Romano cheese, preferably freshly grated
- Salt and ground black pepper, to taste
- 7 eggs, beaten
- 1/2 cup Cotija cheese, grated

Directions

1. Start by adding 1 ½ cups of water and a metal rack to the bottom of the Instant Pot. Spritz each muffin cup with a nonstick cooking spray.
2. Mix the ingredients until everything is well incorporated.
3. Now, spoon the mixture into the lightly greased muffin cups. Lower the cups onto the rack in the Instant Pot.
4. Secure the lid. Choose "Manual" mode and High pressure; cook for 10 minutes. Once cooking is complete, use a natural pressure release; carefully remove the lid. Let cool completely.

Storing

- Place your muffins in the airtight containers or Ziploc bags; keep in the refrigerator for a week.
- For freezing, divide the muffins among three Ziploc bags and freeze up to 3 months. Defrost in your microwave for a couple of minutes. Bon appétit!

10. Asian-Style Savory Egg Custard

Servings 3

Ready in about
15 minutes

NUTRITIONAL
INFORMATION
(Per Serving)

234 - Calories
16.8g - Fat
3.6g - Carbs
16.4g - Protein
1.8g - Sugars

Ingredients

- 3 eggs, well beaten
- 1 cup broth, preferably homemade
- Kosher salt and white pepper, to taste
- 1 tablespoon tamari sauce
- 1/2 tablespoon oyster sauce
- 1/2 cup Comté cheese, grated

Directions

1. Place the beaten eggs in a mixing bowl. Slowly and gradually, add the broth, whisking constantly as you go.
2. Season with salt and paper. Then, pour this mixture through a strainer. Add the tamari sauce and the oyster sauce.
3. Pour the mixture into three ramekins. Now, cover the ramekins with a piece of foil. Place the ramekins on the metal trivet.
4. Secure the lid. Choose "Manual" mode and Low pressure; cook for 7 minutes. Once cooking is complete, use a natural pressure release; carefully remove the lid.
5. Top with the cheese.

Storing

- Divide the custard between thee airtight containers or Ziploc bags. Refrigerate for up to 3 days.
- For freezing, place your custard in three Ziploc bags and freeze up to 3 months. Defrost in the microwave for a few minutes.

11. Bacon and Pepper Casserole with Goat Cheese

Servings 4

Ready in about 30 minutes

NUTRITIONAL INFORMATION (Per Serving)

494 - Calories
41.3g - Fat
5.9g - Carbs
25.5g - Protein
3.5g - Sugars

Ingredients

- 6 ounces bacon, chopped
- 1 green bell pepper, seeded and chopped
- 1 orange bell pepper, seeded and chopped
- 1 Cascabella chili pepper, seeded and minced
- 5 eggs
- 3/4 cup heavy cream
- 6 ounces goat cheese, crumbled
- Sea salt and ground black pepper, to your liking

Directions

1. Add 1 cup of water and a metal trivet to the Instant Pot. Lower the baking pan onto the trivet.
2. Spritz a baking dish that fits inside your Instant Pot with a nonstick cooking spray.
3. Place the bacon on the bottom of the dish. Add the peppers on the top.
4. In a mixing bowl, thoroughly combine the eggs, heavy cream, goat cheese, salt, and black pepper. Spoon this mixture over the top.
5. Secure the lid. Choose "Manual" mode and High pressure; cook for 15 minutes. Once cooking is complete, use a natural pressure release; carefully remove the lid.
6. Allow your casserole to cool for 10 minutes before slicing and serving.

Storing

- Slice the casserole into four pieces. Divide the pieces between airtight containers; it will last for 3 to 4 days in the refrigerator.
- For freezing, place each portion in a separate heavy-duty freezer bag. Freeze up to 2 to 3 months. Defrost in the microwave or refrigerator. Bon appétit!

12. Zingy Habanero Eggs

Servings 4

Ready in about 25 minutes

NUTRITIONAL INFORMATION
(Per Serving)

338 - Calories
25.7g - Fat
5.1g - Carbs
19.8g - Protein
2.8g - Sugars

Ingredients

- 8 eggs
- 2 teaspoons habanero chili pepper, minced
- 1 teaspoon cumin seeds
- 1/4 cup sour cream
- 1/4 cup mayonnaise
- 1 teaspoon stone-ground mustard
- 1/2 teaspoon cayenne pepper
- Sea salt and freshly ground black pepper, to taste

Directions

1. Pour 1 cup of water into the Instant Pot; add a steamer basket to the bottom.
2. Arrange the eggs in the steamer basket.
3. Secure the lid. Choose "Manual" mode and High pressure; cook for 5 minutes. Once cooking is complete, use a natural pressure release; carefully remove the lid.
4. Allow the eggs to cool for 15 minutes. Peel the eggs and separate the egg whites from yolks.
5. Press the "Sauté" button to heat up your Instant Pot; heat the oil. Now, sauté the habanero chili pepper and cumin seeds until they are fragrant.
6. Add the reserved egg yolks to the pepper mixture. Stir in the sour cream, mayonnaise, mustard, cayenne pepper, salt, and black pepper. Now, stuff the egg whites with this mixture.

Storing

- Place the eggs in an airtight container or Ziploc bag; transfer to your refrigerator; they should be consumed within 3 days.
- For freezing, spoon out the yolk mixture from the eggs. Add the egg yolk mixture to an airtight container or Ziploc bag. Place the container in the freezer for up to 3 months.
- To defrost, let them sit overnight in the refrigerator until they are fully thawed out.

13. Rich Pepperoni Pizza Bake

Servings 6

**Ready in about
40 minutes**

**NUTRITIONAL
INFORMATION
(Per Serving)**

421 - Calories
26.7g - Fat
5.7g - Carbs
37.1g - Protein
2.7g - Sugars

Ingredients

- 1 pound ground sirloin
- 1/2 pound ground chuck
- Salt and pepper, to taste
- 1 red bell pepper, sliced
- 1 green bell pepper, sliced
- 1 onion, sliced
- 1 cup mushrooms, sliced
- 1/2 cup Kalamata olives, pitted and halved
- 1 teaspoon basil
- 1 teaspoon oregano
- 1/2 teaspoon rosemary
- 8 ounces tomatoes, diced
- 1 cup pizza sauce
- 1 cup cheddar cheese, shredded
- 1 cup mozzarella cheese, shredded
- 1 cup pepperoni, sliced

Directions

1. Press the "Sauté" button to heat up the Instant Pot. Once hot, cook the beef until nicely browned. Season with salt and pepper to taste.
2. Wipe down the Instant Pot with a damp cloth. Add 1 ½ cups of water and a metal rack to the Instant Pot.
3. Pour the prepared ground meat into a casserole dish that is previously greased with a nonstick cooking spray. Add the bell pepper, onion, mushrooms, and olives.
4. Sprinkle with the basil, oregano, and rosemary. Top with the tomatoes and pizza sauce. Sprinkle evenly with the cheddar and mozzarella cheese.
5. Top with the pepperoni slices. Lower the casserole dish onto the rack. Secure the lid. Choose "Meat/Stew" mode and High pressure; cook for 35 minutes.
6. Once cooking is complete, use a quick pressure release; carefully remove the lid. Let cool completely.

Storing

- Slice the casserole into pieces and place in airtight containers; it will last for 3 to 4 days in the refrigerator.
- For freezing, place the pieces in a separate heavy-duty freezer bag. Freeze up to 2 to 3 months. Defrost in the microwave or refrigerator. Bon appétit!

14. Hangover Seafood Bowl

Servings 6

Ready in about 15 minutes

NUTRITIONAL INFORMATION (Per Serving)

280 - Calories
14g - Fat
4.9g - Carbs
32g - Protein
2.8g - Sugars

Ingredients

- 1 ½ pounds shrimp, peeled and deveined
- 1/2 pound calamari, cleaned
- 1/2 pound lobster
- 2 bay leaves
- 2 rosemary sprigs
- 2 thyme sprigs
- 4 garlic cloves, halved
- 1/2 cup fresh lemon juice
- Sea salt and ground black pepper, to taste
- 3 ripe tomatoes, puréed
- 1/2 cup olives, pitted and halved
- 2 tablespoons fresh coriander, chopped
- 2 tablespoons fresh parsley, chopped
- 3 tablespoons extra-virgin olive oil
- 3 chili peppers, deveined and minced
- 1/2 cup red onion, chopped
- 1 avocado, pitted and sliced

Directions

1. Add the shrimp, calamari, lobster, bay leaves, rosemary, thyme, and garlic to your Instant Pot. Pour in 1 cup of water.
2. Secure the lid. Choose "Manual" mode and Low pressure; cook for 3 minutes. Once cooking is complete, use a quick pressure release; carefully remove the lid.
3. Drain the seafood and transfer to a serving bowl.
4. In a mixing bowl, thoroughly combine the lemon juice, salt, black pepper, tomatoes, olives, coriander, parsley, olive oil, chili peppers, and red onion.
5. Transfer this mixture to the serving bowl with the seafood. Stir to combine well; serve well-chilled, garnished with the avocado.

Storing

- Place all ingredients in airtight containers or Ziploc bags; keep in your refrigerator for up 3 to 4 days.
- Transfer all ingredients to heavy-duty freezer bags. Freeze up to 3 months. Defrost in your refrigerator. Enjoy!

15. Cheesy Cauliflower Balls

Servings 8

Ready in about 25 minutes

NUTRITIONAL INFORMATION (Per Serving)

157 - Calories
12.1g - Fat
3.6g - Carbs
8.9g - Protein
1.2g - Sugars

Ingredients

- 1 head of cauliflower, broken into florets
- 2 tablespoons butter
- Coarse sea salt and white pepper, to taste
- 1/2 teaspoon cayenne pepper
- 1 garlic clove, minced
- 1/2 cup Parmesan cheese, grated
- 1 cup Asiago cheese, shredded
- 2 tablespoons fresh chopped chives, minced
- 2 eggs, beaten

Directions

1. Add 1 cup of water and a steamer basket to the Instant Pot. Now, add the cauliflower to the steamer basket.
2. Secure the lid. Choose "Manual" mode and High pressure; cook for 3 minutes. Once cooking is complete, use a quick pressure release; carefully remove the lid.
3. Transfer the cauliflower to a food processor. Add the remaining ingredients; process until everything is well incorporated.
4. Shape the mixture into balls. Bake in the preheated oven at 400 degrees F for 18 minutes.

Storing

- Transfer the balls to the airtight containers and place in your refrigerator for up to 3 days.
- For freezing, place in freezer safe containers and freeze up to 1 month. Defrost in the microwave for a few minutes. Bon appétit!

16. Golden Cheddar Muffins with Chard

Servings 4

Ready in about
10 minutes

NUTRITIONAL
INFORMATION
(Per Serving)

207 - Calories
14.8g - Fat
4.9g - Carbs
13.4g - Protein
2.7g - Sugars

Ingredients

- 6 eggs
- 4 tablespoons double cream
- Sea salt and ground black pepper, to taste
- 1 cup Swiss chard, chopped
- 1 red bell pepper, chopped
- 1/2 cup white onion, chopped
- 1/2 cup Cheddar cheese, grated

Directions

1. Begin by adding 1 cup of water and a metal rack to the Instant Pot.
2. Mix all of the above ingredients. Then, fill silicone muffin cups about 2/3 full.
3. Then, place the muffin cups on the rack.
4. Secure the lid. Choose "Manual" mode and High pressure; cook for 7 minutes. Once cooking is complete, use a natural pressure release; carefully remove the lid.

Storing

- Place your muffins in the airtight containers or Ziploc bags; keep in the refrigerator for a week.
- For freezing, divide the muffins among three Ziploc bags and freeze up to 3 months. Defrost in your microwave for a couple of minutes. Bon appétit!

17. Special Breakfast Eggs

Servings 3

Ready in about 10 minutes

NUTRITIONAL INFORMATION (Per Serving)

259 - Calories
19.2g - Fat
2g - Carbs
17.9g - Protein
1.3g - Sugars

Ingredients

- 6 large eggs
- Salt and paprika, to taste

Directions

1. Add 1 cup of water and a metal trivet to the Instant Pot.
2. Spritz six silicone cups with a nonstick cooking spray. Crack an egg into each cup.
3. Then, lower the silicone cups onto the metal trivet.
4. Secure the lid. Choose "Steam" mode and High pressure; cook for 4 minutes. Once cooking is complete, use a quick pressure release; carefully remove the lid.
5. Season your eggs with salt and paprika.

Storing

- Place the eggs in three airtight containers; keep in the refrigerator for up 3 to 4 days.
- To freeze, place in separate Ziploc bags and freeze up to 3 months. Defrost in your microwave for a few minutes.

18. Mini Meatloaves with Cheese

Servings 6

Ready in about 20 minutes

NUTRITIONAL INFORMATION (Per Serving)

276 - Calories
17.5g - Fat
3.3g - Carbs
25.6g - Protein
1.7g - Sugars

Ingredients

- 1/2 pound ground pork
- 1/2 pound ground turkey
- 1/2 yellow onion, chopped
- 1/2 cup pork rinds, crushed
- 1 tablespoon coconut aminos
- 2 tablespoons fresh cilantro, chopped
- 3 eggs, whisked
- Sea salt and ground black pepper, to taste
- 1 teaspoon cayenne pepper
- 1/2 teaspoon dried dill weed
- 1/2 teaspoon oregano
- 1 tablespoon mint, chopped
- 1/2 cup pasta sauce, no sugar
- 1/2 cup cheddar cheese, grated

Directions

1. Mix all ingredients, except for the pasta sauce and cheddar cheese, until everything is well incorporated.
2. Now, add 1 cup of water and a metal trivet to the Instant Pot.
3. Divide the mixture among muffin cups; top with the pasta sauce. Lower the muffin cups onto the trivet.
4. Secure the lid. Choose "Manual" mode and High pressure; cook for 6 minutes. Once cooking is complete, use a natural pressure release; carefully remove the lid.
5. Top with the shredded cheese; cover with the lid and allow your muffins to sit in the residual heat for 4 to 7 minutes.
6. Allow the muffins to stand for a few minutes before removing from the cups.

Storing

- Wrap the mini meatloaves tightly with heavy-duty aluminum foil or plastic wrap. Then, keep in your refrigerator for up to 3 to 4 days.
- For freezing, wrap the mini meatloaves tightly to prevent freezer burn. Freeze up to 3 to 4 months. Defrost in the refrigerator. Bon appétit!

19. Garden Omelet with Colby Cheese

Servings 4

Ready in about 15 minutes

NUTRITIONAL INFORMATION (Per Serving)

284 - Calories
24.2g - Fat
4.6g - Carbs
10.5g - Protein
2.4g - Sugars

Ingredients

- 2 tablespoons olive oil
- 1 yellow onion, chopped
- 1 zucchini, sliced
- 2 garlic cloves, minced
- 4 eggs, beaten
- 4 tablespoons heavy whipped cream
- Sea salt and ground black pepper, to taste
- 1 teaspoon cayenne pepper
- 1 tablespoon Cajun seasoning
- 1/2 cup Colby cheese, shredded

Directions

1. Press the "Sauté" button to heat up your Instant Pot. Heat the oil and sauté the onion until tender and translucent.
2. Now, add the zucchini and garlic and cook for 1 minute more.
3. Thoroughly combine the eggs, heavy whipped cream, salt, black pepper, cayenne pepper, and Cajun seasoning. Add the egg mixture to the Instant Pot.
4. Secure the lid. Choose "Manual" mode and High pressure; cook for 6 minutes. Once cooking is complete, use a quick pressure release; carefully remove the lid.
5. Add the shredded cheese and put the lid on the Instant Pot. Let it sit in the residual heat for 4 minutes.

Storing

- Slice the omelet into four pieces and place each of them in an airtight container or Ziploc bag; keep in your refrigerator for up 3 to 4 days.
- To freeze, place in separate Ziploc bags and freeze up to 3 months. Defrost in your microwave for a few minutes. Bon appétit!

20. Winter Bacon and Leek Quiche

Servings 6

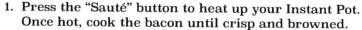

Ready in about 35 minutes

NUTRITIONAL INFORMATION (Per Serving)

231 - Calories
15.2g - Fat
4.8g - Carbs
16.5g - Protein
3.1g - Sugars

Ingredients

- 4 slices Canadian bacon, chopped
- 1 cup leeks, chopped
- 1 garlic clove, minced
- 8 eggs
- 1/2 cup half-and-half
- 1/2 cup cream cheese, room temperature
- Seasoned salt and ground black pepper, to taste
- 1 tablespoon dried sage, crushed
- 1/2 teaspoon marjoram
- 1/2 cup Swiss cheese, freshly grated

Directions

1. Press the "Sauté" button to heat up your Instant Pot. Once hot, cook the bacon until crisp and browned.
2. Add the leeks and garlic and cook 1 minute more. Add the eggs, half-and-half, cream cheese, salt, black pepper, sage and marjoram.
3. Grease a baking pan with a nonstick cooking spray. Spoon the bacon/egg mixture into the prepared baking pan.
4. Now, add 1 cup of water and a metal trivet to the Instant Pot; lower the baking pan onto the trivet.
5. Secure the lid. Choose "Meat/Stew" mode and High pressure; cook for 25 minutes. Once cooking is complete, use a quick pressure release; carefully remove the lid.
6. Add the Swiss cheese and cover with the lid; let it sit in the residual heat for 5 minutes.

Storing

- Slice the quiche into six pieces; divide between airtight containers or Ziploc bags; keep in your refrigerator for up to 3 days.
- For freezing, place them in airtight containers or heavy-duty freezer bags. Freeze up to 3 months. Once thawed in the refrigerator, heat in the microwave until warmed through. Enjoy!

LUNCH

21. Family Cauliflower Soup

Servings 4

Ingredients

- 4 tablespoons butter, softened
- 1/2 cup leeks, thinly sliced
- 2 cloves garlic, minced
- 3/4 pound cauliflower, broken into florets
- 1 cup water
- 2 cups chicken stock
- 1 cup full-fat milk
- Kosher salt, to taste
- 1/3 teaspoon ground black pepper

Ready in about 10 minutes

Directions

1. Press the "Sauté" button to heat up your Instant Pot. Then, melt the butter; sauté the leeks until softened.
2. Then, sauté the garlic until fragrant, about 30 seconds. Add the remaining ingredients and gently stir to combine.
3. Secure the lid. Choose "Manual" mode and Low pressure; cook for 5 minutes. Once cooking is complete, use a quick pressure release; carefully remove the lid.
4. Let cool completely before storing.

NUTRITIONAL INFORMATION (Per Serving)

167 - Calories
13.7g - Fat
5.4g - Carbs
3.8g - Protein
5.1g - Sugars

Storing

- Spoon the soup into four airtight containers; keep in your refrigerator for up 3 to 4 days.
- For freezing, place it in airtight containers or heavy-duty freezer bags. Freeze up to 4 to 6 months. Defrost in the microwave or refrigerator. Enjoy!

22. Buffalo Thick Pork Soup

Servings 4

Ready in about
20 minutes

NUTRITIONAL
INFORMATION
(Per Serving)

443 - Calories
32.7g - Fat
3.7g - Carbs
32.6g - Protein
1.9g - Sugars

Ingredients

- 2 tablespoons butter
- 1 pound pork loin, boneless and cubed
- 1/2 cup celery, diced
- 1 tablespoon hot sauce
- 1/3 cup blue cheese powder
- Seasoned salt and ground black pepper, to taste
- 1/2 teaspoon onion powder
- 1/2 teaspoon garlic powder
- 1 teaspoon paprika
- 1/4 teaspoon dried dill weed
- 4 cups beef bone stock
- 1 cup heavy cream

Directions

1. Press the "Sauté" button to heat up the Instant Pot. Now, melt the butter and cook the pork loin for 2 to 4 minutes, stirring frequently.
2. Add the celery, hot sauce, blue cheese powder, salt, pepper, onion powder, garlic powder, paprika, dill, and beef bone stock.
3. Secure the lid. Choose "Manual" mode and High pressure; cook for 12 minutes. Once cooking is complete, use a quick pressure release; carefully remove the lid.
4. Add the heavy cream and press the "Sauté" button one more time. Let the soup simmer until thickened. Let cool completely before storing.

Storing

- Spoon the soup into four airtight containers or Ziploc bags; keep in your refrigerator for up to 3 to 4 days.
- For freezing, place the soup in airtight containers. Freeze up to 4 to 6 months. Defrost in the refrigerator. Bon appétit!

23. Hot Spicy Chicken Soup

Servings 5

Ready in about 20 minutes

NUTRITIONAL INFORMATION (Per Serving)

238 - Calories
17g - Fat
5.4g - Carbs
16.4g - Protein
2.6g - Sugars

Ingredients

- 2 tablespoons grapeseed oil
- 2 banana shallots, chopped
- 4 cloves garlic, minced
- 1 cup Cremini mushrooms, sliced
- 2 bell peppers, seeded and sliced
- 1 serrano pepper, seeded and sliced
- 2 ripe tomatoes, pureed
- 1 teaspoon porcini powder
- 2 tablespoons dry white wine
- Sea salt and ground black pepper, to your liking
- 1 teaspoon dried basil
- 1/2 teaspoon dried dill weed
- 5 cups broth, preferably homemade
- 4 chicken wings

Directions

1. Press the "Sauté" button and heat the oil. Once hot, sauté the shallots until just tender and aromatic.
2. Add the garlic, mushrooms, and peppers; cook an additional 3 minutes or until softened.
3. Now, stir in the tomatoes, porcini powder, white wine, salt, and black pepper. Add the remaining ingredients and stir to combine.
4. Secure the lid. Choose "Manual" mode and High pressure; cook for 18 minutes. Once cooking is complete, use a quick pressure release.
5. Make sure to release any remaining steam and carefully remove the lid. Remove the chicken wings from the Instant Pot. Discard the bones and chop the meat.
6. Add the chicken meat back to the Instant Pot.

Storing

- Spoon the soup into five airtight containers or Ziploc bags; keep in your refrigerator for up to 3 to 4 days.
- For freezing, place the soup in airtight containers. It will maintain the best quality for about 4 to 6 months. Defrost in the refrigerator. Bon appétit!

24. The Best Ever Chicken Goulash

Servings 6

Ready in about 25 minutes

NUTRITIONAL INFORMATION (Per Serving)

353 - Calories
19.5g - Fat
5.9g - Carbs
34.3g - Protein
3.3g - Sugars

Ingredients

- 1 tablespoon olive oil
- 2 pounds chicken breast halves, boneless and skinless
- 2 small-sized shallots, chopped
- 1 teaspoon garlic paste
- 1 cup milk
- 2 ripe tomatoes, chopped
- 1 teaspoon curry powder
- 1 tablespoon tamari sauce
- 1 tablespoon balsamic vinegar
- 2 tablespoons vermouth
- Sea salt, to taste
- 1/2 teaspoon cayenne pepper
- 1/3 teaspoon black pepper
- 1/2 teaspoon hot paprika
- 1/2 teaspoon ginger, freshly grated
- 1 celery stalk with leaves, chopped
- 1 bell pepper, chopped
- 1 tablespoon flaxseed meal

Directions

1. Press the "Sauté" button to heat up the Instant Pot. Now, add olive oil. Once hot, sear the chicken breast halves for 3 to 4 minutes per side.
2. Add the shallots, garlic, milk, tomatoes, curry powder, tamari sauce, vinegar, vermouth, salt, cayenne pepper, black pepper, hot paprika, ginger, celery and bell pepper to the Instant Pot; stir to combine well.
3. Secure the lid. Choose the "Meat/Stew" setting and cook for 20 minutes at High pressure. Once cooking is complete, use a quick pressure release; carefully remove the lid.
4. Add the flaxseed meal and continue stirring in the residual heat. Let cool completely before storing.

Storing

- Spoon the goulash into airtight containers; keep in your refrigerator for 3 to 4 days.
- For freezing, place the goulash in airtight containers or heavy-duty freezer bags. It will maintain the best quality for about 4 to 6 months.
- Defrost in the microwave or refrigerator. Bon appétit!

25. Pork Cutlets with Porcini Mushroom Sauce

Servings 4

Ready in about 15 minutes

NUTRITIONAL INFORMATION
(Per Serving)

412 - Calories
25.4g - Fat
2.1g - Carbs
41.5g - Protein
0.8g - Sugars

Ingredients

- 2 teaspoons olive oil
- 4 pork cutlets
- Seasoned salt to taste
- 1/2 teaspoon ground black pepper
- 1/2 teaspoon cayenne pepper
- 1/2 cup scallions, chopped
- 1 cup Porcini mushrooms, thinly sliced
- 1 teaspoon roasted garlic paste
- 1 bay leaf
- 1 cup broth, preferably homemade
- 1 tablespoon arrowroot powder + 1 tablespoon water
- 1/2 cup heavy cream

Directions

1. Press the "Sauté" button to heat up the Instant Pot; add the olive oil.
2. Now, sear the pork cutlets until delicately browned on both sides. Season with salt, black pepper, and cayenne pepper.
3. Then, add the scallions, mushrooms, garlic paste, bay leaf, and broth to the Instant Pot.
4. Secure the lid. Choose the "Manual" setting and cook for 10 minutes under High pressure. Once cooking is complete, use a quick pressure release; carefully remove the lid.
5. Now, whisk the arrowroot powder with 1 tablespoon of water in a small mixing bowl. Add this slurry along with the heavy cream to the cooking liquid.
6. Press the "Sauté" button again to thicken the cooking liquid.
7. Let cool completely.

Storing

- Divide the pork cutlets and sauce into four portions; place each portion in a separate airtight container or Ziploc bag; keep in your refrigerator for 3 to 4 days.
- Freeze the pork cutlets in sauce in airtight containers or heavy-duty freezer bags. Freeze up to 4 months. Defrost in the refrigerator. Bon appétit!

26. Beef Stew with a Twist

Servings 6

Ready in about
25 minutes

NUTRITIONAL
INFORMATION
(Per Serving)

317 - Calories
15.3g - Fat
5.7g - Carbs
40g - Protein
2.1g - Sugars

Ingredients

- 1 tablespoon tallow, room temperature
- 1 ½ pounds beef stew meat, cubed
- 2 slices bacon, chopped
- 1 parsnip, chopped
- 1 carrot, chopped
- 1 celery with leaves, chopped
- 1/2 cup leeks, chopped
- 2 cloves garlic, chopped
- 1 sprig thyme, chopped
- 1 sprig rosemary, chopped
- 2 bay leaves
- 3 cups water
- 1 teaspoon cayenne pepper
- 1/2 teaspoon Hungarian paprika
- Salt and ground black pepper, to taste
- 2 cups spinach, torn into pieces

Directions

1. Press the "Sauté" button to heat up the Instant Pot. Now, melt the tallow until hot; cook the beef for 2 to 3 minutes, stirring frequently.
2. Add the remaining ingredients, except for the spinach, and stir to combine well.
3. Secure the lid. Choose "Meat/Stew" mode and High pressure; cook for 20 minutes. Once cooking is complete, use a natural pressure release; carefully remove the lid.
4. Add the spinach to the Instant Pot; cover it with the lid and let the spinach wilt. Let cool completely.

Storing

- Spoon your stew into airtight containers; keep in your refrigerator for 3 to 4 days.
- For freezing, place your stew in airtight containers or heavy-duty freezer bags. It will maintain the best quality for about 4 to 6 months.
- Defrost in the microwave or refrigerator. Bon appétit!

27. Winter Beef Soup

Servings 6

Ready in about 20 minutes

NUTRITIONAL INFORMATION (Per Serving)

239 - Calories
14.2g - Fat
4.5g - Carbs
24g - Protein
1.6g - Sugars

Ingredients

- 2 tablespoons butter, at room temperature
- 1 ½ pounds beef short ribs
- 6 cups water
- 2 cloves garlic, smashed
- 1 cup scallions, chopped
- 1 carrot, chopped
- 1 celery, chopped
- 3 beef stock cubes
- Kosher salt and ground black pepper, to taste
- 1 cup Swiss chard, torn into pieces

Directions

1. Press the "Sauté" button to heat up the Instant Pot. Then, melt the butter; once hot, cook the ribs for 2 to 4 minutes on each side.
2. Add the water, garlic, scallions, carrot, celery, beef stock cube, salt, and black pepper to the Instant Pot.
3. Choose "Manual" mode and High pressure; cook for 15 minutes. Once cooking is complete, use a natural pressure release; carefully remove the lid.
4. Add the Swiss chard, cover with the lid and allow the greens to wilt completely. Let cool completely.

Storing

- Spoon the soup into airtight containers; keep in your refrigerator for up to 4 days.
- For freezing, place the soup in airtight containers or heavy-duty freezer bags. Freeze up to 4 to 6 months. Defrost in the microwave or refrigerator. Bon appétit!

28. The Best Pork Chile Verde

Servings 6

Ready in about
25 minutes

NUTRITIONAL
INFORMATION
(Per Serving)

358 - Calories
19.2g - Fat
4.5g - Carbs
39.7g - Protein
2.1g - Sugars

Ingredients

- 1 tablespoon olive oil
- 2 pounds Boston butt, trimmed, cut into cubes
- 2 tomatoes, diced
- 1 cup water
- 1/2 cup mild green chilies, roasted, seeded and diced
- 1 red bell pepper, seeded and chopped
- 1/2 cup green onions, chopped
- 3 cloves garlic, peeled and halved
- 1 teaspoon cumin, ground
- 1 teaspoon dried Mexican oregano
- Kosher salt and ground black pepper, to taste
- 1 teaspoon red pepper flakes
- 2 tablespoons fresh cilantro leaves, chopped

Directions

1. Press the "Sauté" button to heat up the Instant Pot. Heat the oil until sizzling. Then, sear the Boston butt for 2 to 4 minutes, stirring frequently.
2. Add the other ingredients, except for the cilantro leaves.
3. Secure the lid. Choose the "Meat/Stew" setting and cook for 20 minutes under High pressure. Once cooking is complete, use a natural pressure release; carefully remove the lid; reserve the pork.
4. Add the cilantro to the cooking liquid. Blitz the mixture in your food processor until creamy and uniform. Return the pork to the Instant Pot.
5. Let cool completely.

Storing

- Spoon the Pork Chile Verde into airtight containers or Ziploc bags; keep in your refrigerator for up to 3 to 4 days.
- For freezing, place the Pork Chile Verde in airtight containers. Freeze up to 4 to 6 months. Defrost in the refrigerator. Bon appétit!

29. Creamy Turkey Breasts with Mushrooms

Servings 6

Ready in about 15 minutes

NUTRITIONAL INFORMATION (Per Serving)

248 - Calories
13.9g - Fat
3.3g - Carbs
26.1g - Protein
1.6g - Sugars

Ingredients

- 3 teaspoons butter
- 1 ½ pounds turkey breasts, cubed
- 1 cup white mushrooms, thinly sliced
- 2 cloves garlic, minced
- 1/2 leek, chopped
- 1/2 cup broth, preferably homemade
- Salt and black pepper, to taste
- 1/4 teaspoon ground allspice
- 1/2 teaspoon basil
- 1/2 teaspoon dried parsley flakes
- 1 teaspoon porcini powder
- 1/2 cup double cream

Directions

1. Press the "Sauté" button and melt the butter. Now, sear the turkey for 3 to 4 minutes, stirring constantly; set aside.
2. Add the mushrooms, garlic and leeks and cook in pan drippings until aromatic and just tender. Add the broth and aromatics.
3. Now, secure the lid. Choose the "Manual" setting and cook for 8 minutes under High pressure. Once cooking is complete, use a quick pressure release; carefully remove the lid.
4. Add the double cream and cook in the residual heat until thoroughly warmed. Let cool completely.

Storing

- Place the turkey breast with sauce in airtight containers; keep in your refrigerator for up to 3 to 4 days.
- For freezing, place the turkey breast with sauce in airtight containers or heavy-duty freezer bags. Freeze up to 2 to 3 months. Defrost in the refrigerator. Bon appétit!

30. Chicken Legs in Mustard Curry Sauce

Servings 5

Ready in about 25 minutes

NUTRITIONAL INFORMATION (Per Serving)

477 - Calories
26.1g - Fat
4.5g - Carbs
52.8g - Protein
1.4g - Sugars

Ingredients

- 5 chicken legs, boneless, skin-on
- 2 garlic cloves, halved
- Sea salt, to taste
- 1/4 teaspoon black pepper, preferably freshly ground
- 1/2 teaspoon smoked paprika
- 2 teaspoons olive oil
- 1 tablespoon yellow mustard
- 1 teaspoon curry paste
- 4 strips pancetta, chopped
- 1 shallot, peeled and chopped
- 1 cup roasted vegetable broth, preferably homemade

Directions

1. Rub the chicken legs with garlic halves; then, season with salt, black pepper, and smoked paprika.
2. Press the "Sauté" button to heat up your Instant Pot.
3. Once hot, heat the oil and sauté the chicken legs for 4 to 5 minutes, turning once during cooking. Add a splash of chicken broth to deglaze the bottom of the pan.
4. Spread the legs with mustard and curry paste. Add the pancetta, shallot and remaining vegetable broth.
5. Secure the lid. Choose "Manual" mode and High pressure; cook for 14 minutes. Once cooking is complete, use a natural pressure release; carefully remove the lid.

Storing

- Place the chicken legs along with the sauce in airtight containers or Ziploc bags; keep in your refrigerator for up to 3 to 4 days.
- For freezing, place them in airtight containers or heavy-duty freezer bags. Freeze up to 3 months. Once thawed in the refrigerator, heat in the preheated oven at 375 degrees F for 20 to 25 minutes. Bon appétit!

31. Gruyère and Turkey Au Gratin

Servings 4

Ready in about 40 minutes

NUTRITIONAL INFORMATION (Per Serving)

540 - Calories
35g - Fat
2.9g - Carbs
51.8g - Protein
1.8g - Sugars

Ingredients

- 1 tablespoon canola oil
- 1 pound turkey legs, boneless and skinless
- 6 ounces smoked deli ham
- 8 ounces Cottage cheese
- 1/2 teaspoon mustard powder
- 1/3 teaspoon cayenne pepper, or more to taste
- 1 cup water
- 2 cups Gruyère cheese, shredded (or another cheese of your choice)
- Salt and ground black pepper, to taste

Directions

1. Press the "Sauté" button to heat up the Instant Pot. Now, heat the oil and cook the turkey legs until no longer pink.
2. Add the ham, Cottage cheese, mustard powder, cayenne pepper, and water; gently stir to combine.
3. Secure the lid. Choose the "Meat/Stew" setting and cook for 35 minutes under High pressure. Once cooking is complete, use a natural pressure release; carefully remove the lid.
4. Add the shredded cheese and continue to cook in the residual heat until the cheese has melted completely.
5. Season with salt and black pepper; taste, adjust the seasonings. Let cool completely.

Storing

- Cut this Au Gratin into four pieces. Place each piece in a separate airtight container or Ziploc bag; keep for 3 to 4 days in the refrigerator.
- To freeze, place each piece in a separate heavy-duty freezer bag. Freeze up to 2 to 3 months. Defrost in the microwave or refrigerator. Bon appétit!

32. Cheesy Chicken and Mushroom Casserole

Servings 4

Ready in about 15 minutes

NUTRITIONAL INFORMATION (Per Serving)

469 - Calories
32.3g - Fat
6.1g - Carbs
36.3g - Protein
4.2g - Sugars

Ingredients

- 1 tablespoon lard
- 1 pound chicken breasts, cubed
- 10 ounces button mushrooms, thinly sliced
- 2 cloves garlic, smashed
- 1/2 cup yellow onion, chopped
- 1/2 teaspoon turmeric powder
- 1/2 teaspoon shallot powder
- 1/2 teaspoon dried sage
- 1/2 teaspoon dried basil
- Kosher salt, to taste
- 1/2 teaspoon cayenne pepper
- 1/3 teaspoon ground black pepper
- 1 cup chicken broth
- 1/2 cup double cream
- 1 cup Colby cheese, shredded

Directions

1. Press the "Sauté" button to heat up the Instant Pot. Now, melt the lard and cook the chicken, mushrooms, garlic, and onion; cook until the vegetables are softened.
2. Add the turmeric powder, shallot powder, sage, basil, salt, cayenne pepper, black pepper, and broth.
3. Secure the lid. Choose the "Meat/Stew" setting and cook for 6 minutes at High pressure. Once cooking is complete, use a natural pressure release; carefully remove the lid.
4. Now, add the double cream and cook in the residual heat until thoroughly heated.
5. Top with cheese and bake in the preheated oven at 390 degrees F until the cheese is bubbling. Let cool completely.

Storing

- Cut this casserole into four pieces. Place each piece in a separate airtight container or Ziploc bag; keep for 3 to 4 days in the refrigerator.
- To freeze, place each piece in a separate heavy-duty freezer bag. Freeze up to 2 to 3 months. Defrost in the microwave or refrigerator. Bon appétit!

33. Greek-Style Pork Stew

Servings 8

Ready in about 15 minutes

NUTRITIONAL INFORMATION (Per Serving)

249 - Calories
10.1g - Fat
5.1g - Carbs
31.2g - Protein
2.7g - Sugars

Ingredients

- 1 tablespoon olive oil
- 2 ½ pounds pork stew meat, cubed
- 1 red onion, chopped
- 4 cloves garlic, peeled
- 1 bell pepper, chopped
- 2 tablespoons Greek red wine
- 1 cup beef bone broth
- 1 star anise
- Coarse sea salt and ground black pepper, to taste
- 1 teaspoon dried basil
- 1 teaspoon dried oregano
- 1/2 teaspoon dried dill weed
- 1 (14.5-ounce) can diced tomatoes
- 2 tablespoons fresh basil leaves, snipped

Directions

1. Press the "Sauté" button to heat up the Instant Pot. Heat the olive oil and sauté the meat until browned; reserve.
2. Then, in pan drippings, cook the onion, garlic, and bell pepper until softened. Add the red wine to deglaze the pan.
3. Add the beef bone broth, star anise, sea salt, black pepper, dried basil, oregano, dill and canned tomatoes.
4. Secure the lid. Choose the "Manual" setting and cook for 10 minutes under High pressure. Once cooking is complete, use a quick pressure release; carefully remove the lid.
5. Add fresh basil leaves. Let cool completely.

Storing

- Spoon the pork stew into airtight containers or Ziploc bags; keep in your refrigerator for up to 3 to 4 days.
- For freezing, place the pork stew in airtight containers. Freeze up to 4 to 6 months. Defrost in the refrigerator. Bon appétit!

34. Beef Medley with Sausage

Servings 8

Ready in about 30 minutes

NUTRITIONAL INFORMATION (Per Serving)

319 - Calories
14g - Fat
5.3g - Carbs
42.8g - Protein
1.8g - Sugars

Ingredients

- 1 teaspoon tallow
- 2 beef sausages, casing removed and sliced
- 2 pounds beef steak, cubed
- 1 yellow onion, sliced
- 2 cloves garlic, minced
- 1 red bell pepper, chopped
- 1 jalapeño pepper, chopped
- Sea salt and ground black pepper, to taste
- 1/2 teaspoon paprika
- 1 teaspoon old bay seasoning
- 1 sprig rosemary
- 2 bay leaves
- 1 sprig thyme
- 2 fresh ripe tomatoes, puréed
- 1 ½ cups roasted vegetable broth

Directions

1. Press the "Sauté" button to heat up the Instant Pot. Then, melt the tallow and cook the sausage and steak for 3 to 4 minutes, stirring periodically; reserve.
2. Now, add the onion; sauté the onion until softened and translucent. Add the remaining ingredients, including the reserved beef and sausage.
3. Secure the lid. Choose "Manual" mode and High pressure; cook for 20 minutes. Once cooking is complete, use a quick pressure release; carefully remove the lid.
4. Let cool completely.

Storing

- Spoon the medley into airtight containers; keep in your refrigerator for 3 to 4 days.
- For freezing, place the medley in airtight containers or heavy-duty freezer bags. Freeze up to 4 months. Defrost in the microwave. Bon appétit!

35. Thick Flank Steak Chili

Servings 6

Ready in about 20 minutes

NUTRITIONAL INFORMATION (Per Serving)

268 - Calories
10.2g - Fat
6g - Carbs
34.1g - Protein
4.3g - Sugars

Ingredients

- 1 tablespoon grapeseed oil
- 2 pounds beef flank steak, cubed
- 1 jalapeño pepper, seeded and diced
- 2 shallots, diced
- 1 celery stalk, diced
- 2 Romano tomatoes, puréed
- Coarse sea salt and ground black pepper, to your liking
- 2 tablespoons fresh coriander, coarsely chopped
- 1 tablespoon coconut aminos
- 1 tablespoon Kashmiri chili powder
- 1/2 teaspoon smoked cayenne pepper
- 1/2 teaspoon red pepper flakes, crushed
- 1/3 cup fresh chives, chopped

Directions

1. Press the "Sauté" button to heat up the Instant Pot. Now, heat the oil. Once hot, cook the beef for 3 minutes per side or until it is delicately browned.
2. Add the other ingredients, except for the fresh chives. Add 1 cup of water and stir.
3. Secure the lid. Choose "Manual" mode and High pressure; cook for 15 minutes. Once cooking is complete, use a natural pressure release; carefully remove the lid.
4. Garnish with fresh chives. Let cool completely.

Storing

- Spoon the chili into airtight containers; keep in your refrigerator for 3 to 4 days.
- For freezing, place the chili in airtight containers or heavy-duty freezer bags. Freeze up to 4 months. Defrost in the microwave. Bon appétit!

36. Mediterranean Pork Cutlets

Servings 6

Ingredients

- 3 tablespoons olive oil
- 1 lemon, juiced
- 2 garlic cloves, finely minced
- 1 bunch of fresh cilantro leaves, chopped
- 1 tablespoons stone ground mustard
- 2 sprigs fresh rosemary, chopped
- 1 sprig lemon thyme, chopped
- 2 pounds pork cutlets, bone-in
- Coarse sea salt and ground black pepper, to taste
- 1/4 cup white rum
- 1 cup chicken stock
- 1/2 cup black olives, pitted and sliced

Ready in about 3 hours 15 minutes

Directions

1. Add 2 tablespoons of olive oil, lemon juice, garlic, cilantro, mustard, rosemary, and lemon thyme to a ceramic dish.
2. Add the bone-in pork cutlets and let them marinate at least 3 hours or overnight.
3. Press the "Sauté" button to heat up the Instant Pot. Now, heat the remaining tablespoon of olive oil and brown the pork for 2 to 4 minutes or until delicately browned on each side.
4. Season with salt and pepper to taste.
5. Deglaze the bottom of the inner pot with the white rum until it has almost all evaporated. Pour in the stock.
6. Secure the lid. Choose "Manual" mode and High pressure; cook for 8 minutes. Once cooking is complete, use a quick pressure release; carefully remove the lid.
7. Garnish with black olives. Let cool completely.

Storing

- Divide the pork cutlets into six portions; place each portion in a separate airtight container or Ziploc bag; keep in your refrigerator for 3 to 4 days.
- Freeze the pork cutlets in airtight containers or heavy-duty freezer bags. Freeze up to 4 months.
- Remove the pork cutlets from the freezer and place them in the refrigerator. Reheat the pork cutlets in the same way you prepared them, if possible.

**NUTRITIONAL INFORMATION
(Per Serving)**

417 - Calories
25.7g - Fat
4.6g - Carbs
40.4g - Protein
1.5g - Sugars

37. Ground Pork Taco Bowl

Servings 6

Ready in about
15 minutes

NUTRITIONAL
INFORMATION
(Per Serving)

271 - Calories
11.2g - Fat
5g - Carbs
36.1g - Protein
3.1g - Sugars

Ingredients

- 1 teaspoon olive oil
- 2 pounds lean ground pork
- 1 cup chicken bone stock
- 3 ounces dried guajillo chilies, seeded, roasted and minced
- 1/2 cup yellow onions, chopped
- 2 cloves garlic, chopped
- 1 teaspoon dried Mexican oregano
- 1/2 teaspoon ground coriander
- Sea salt and ground black pepper, to taste
- 1 teaspoon cayenne pepper
- 1/2 teaspoon sweet paprika
- 1 cup cherry tomatoes, halved
- 1 tablespoon fresh lime juice
- 1/2 cup Cheddar cheese, shredded

Directions

1. Press the "Sauté" button to heat up the Instant Pot. Heat the olive oil and brown the pork, crumbling with a spatula.
2. Use the chicken bone stock to deglaze the pan. Now, add the dried guajillo chilies, yellow onions, garlic, Mexican oregano, ground coriander, salt, black pepper, cayenne pepper, sweet paprika, and tomatoes.
3. Secure the lid. Choose the "Manual" setting and cook for 5 minutes at High pressure. Once cooking is complete, use a natural pressure release; carefully remove the lid.
4. Drizzle with some fresh lime juice and top with the shredded cheese. Let cool completely.

Storing

- Place the ground pork mixture in airtight containers or Ziploc bags; keep in your refrigerator for up to 3 to 4 days.
- For freezing, place the ground pork mixture in airtight containers or heavy-duty freezer bags. Freeze up to 2 to 3 months. Defrost in the refrigerator. Bon appétit!

38. Favorite Beef Paprikash

Servings 6

Ready in about 25 minutes

NUTRITIONAL INFORMATION (Per Serving)

271 - Calories
11.3g - Fat
5.1g - Carbs
35.1g - Protein
2.8g - Sugars

Ingredients

- 2 teaspoons grapeseed oil
- 2 pounds beef steak cubes
- Salt and ground black pepper, to your liking
- 1 tablespoon sweet paprika
- 1/2 tablespoon hot paprika
- 1 tablespoon fish sauce
- 2 cloves garlic, minced
- 1/2 cup leeks, chopped
- 1 bell pepper, seeded and sliced
- 2 carrots, sliced
- 1 celery with leaves, diced
- 2 cups chicken stock
- 1/2 cup water
- 2 tomatoes, puréed
- 1 tablespoon flaxseed meal plus 1 ½ tablespoons water

Directions

1. Press the "Sauté" button to heat up the Instant Pot. Heat the oil and cook the beef until no longer pink. Season with salt and pepper to taste.
2. Add the paprika, fish sauce, garlic, leeks, bell pepper, carrots and celery to the Instant Pot. Pour in the chicken stock, water, and puréed tomatoes.
3. Secure the lid. Choose "Manual" mode and High pressure; cook for 20 minutes. Once cooking is complete, use a natural pressure release; carefully remove the lid.
4. Then, mix the flaxseed meal with the water to make the slurry. Add the slurry to the cooking liquid, stir well and cover with the lid. Let cool completely.

Storing

- Spoon the Beef Paprikash into airtight containers; keep in your refrigerator for up to 4 days.
- For freezing, place the Beef Paprikash in airtight containers or heavy-duty freezer bags. Freeze up to 4 to 6 months. Defrost in the microwave or refrigerator. Bon appétit!

39. The Best Fish Chili

Servings 4

Ready in about 10 minutes

NUTRITIONAL INFORMATION (Per Serving)

213 - Calories
12.7g - Fat
5.9g - Carbs
17.1g - Protein
2.9g - Sugars

Ingredients

- 2 tablespoons olive oil
- 1 red onion, coarsely chopped
- 1 teaspoon ginger-garlic paste
- 1 celery stalk, diced
- 1 carrot, sliced
- 1 bell pepper, deveined and thinly sliced
- 1 jalapeño pepper, deveined and minced
- 2 ripe Roma tomatoes, crushed
- 1/2 pound snapper, sliced
- 1/2 cup water
- 1/2 cup broth, preferably homemade
- 2 tablespoons fresh coriander, minced
- Sea salt and ground black pepper, to taste
- 1/2 teaspoon cayenne pepper
- 1 bay leaf
- 1/4 teaspoon dried dill
- 1/2 cup Cheddar cheese, grated

Directions

1. Press the "Sauté" button to heat up your Instant Pot. Now, heat the olive oil and cook the onion until translucent and tender.
2. Now, add the remaining ingredients, except for the grated Cheddar cheese.
3. Secure the lid. Choose "Manual" mode and High pressure; cook for 6 minutes. Once cooking is complete, use a quick pressure release; carefully remove the lid.
4. Garnish with the grated Cheddar cheese. Let cool completely.

Storing

- Spoon the fish chili into airtight containers; it will last for 3 to 4 days in the refrigerator.
- For freezing, place the fish chili in airtight containers or heavy-duty freezer bags. Freeze up to 4 to 6 months. Defrost in the microwave or refrigerator. Bon appétit!

40. Chicken Parm Chowder

Servings 6

Ready in about 40 minutes

NUTRITIONAL INFORMATION (Per Serving)

405 - Calories
18.4g - Fat
4.7g - Carbs
50.1g - Protein
1.1g - Sugars

Ingredients

- 2 pounds whole chicken, cut into pieces
- 3 ounces full-fat milk
- 1 teaspoon fresh lemon juice
- 1/2 teaspoon fresh ginger, grated
- 2 garlic cloves, minced
- 4 ounces cottage cheese, at room temperature
- 2 banana shallots, peeled and chopped
- 1 carrot, chopped
- 2 tablespoons butter
- 1 tablespoon dried rosemary
- 1/4 teaspoon ground black pepper
- Sea salt, to taste
- 4 cups chicken stock, low-sodium
- 1/2 cup Parmesan cheese, preferably freshly grated
- 1 tablespoon fresh parsley, chopped

Directions

1. In a mixing bowl, place the chicken pieces, milk, lemon juice, ginger, and garlic; let it marinate for 1 hour in the refrigerator.
2. Add the chicken, along with the marinade, to your Instant Pot. Add the cottage cheese, shallots, carrot, butter, rosemary, black pepper, salt, and chicken stock.
3. Secure the lid. Press the "Soup" button and cook for 35 minutes. Once cooking is complete, use a quick pressure release.
4. Remove the chicken from the cooking liquid. Discard the bones and add the chicken back to the Instant Pot.
5. Add the freshly grated Parmesan cheese to the hot cooking liquid; stir until it is melted and everything is well combined. Garnish with fresh parsley. Let cool completely.

Storing

- Spoon the chicken parm chowder into airtight containers or Ziploc bags; keep in your refrigerator for up to 3 to 4 days.
- For freezing, place the chicken parm chowder in airtight containers. It will maintain the best quality for about 4 to 6 months. Defrost in the refrigerator. Bon appétit!

DINNER

41. Chicken Liver Pâté

Servings 8

Ingredients

- 1 pound chicken livers
- 1/2 cup leeks, chopped
- 2 garlic cloves, crushed
- 2 tablespoons olive oil
- 1 tablespoon poultry seasonings
- 1 teaspoon dried rosemary
- 1/2 teaspoon dried marjoram
- 1/4 teaspoon dried dill weed
- 1/2 teaspoon paprika
- 1/2 teaspoon red pepper flakes
- Salt, to taste
- 1/2 teaspoon ground black pepper
- 1 cup water
- 1 tablespoon stone ground mustard

Ready in about 15 minutes

Directions

1. Press the "Sauté" button to heat up the Instant Pot. Now, heat the oil.
2. Once hot, sauté the chicken livers until no longer pink.
3. Add the remaining ingredients, except for the mustard, to your Instant Pot.
4. Secure the lid. Choose the "Manual" setting and cook for 10 minutes at High pressure. Once cooking is complete, use a quick pressure release; carefully remove the lid.
5. Transfer the cooked mixture to a food processor; add the stone ground mustard. Process until smooth and uniform.
6. Let cool completely.

NUTRITIONAL INFORMATION (Per Serving)

109 - Calories
6.5g - Fat
2.3g - Carbs
10g - Protein
0.3g - Sugars

Storing

- Spoon the liver pâté into airtight containers or Ziploc bags; keep in your refrigerator for up to 6 days.
- Wrap the chicken liver pate in a plastic wrap. If you wanted to use small serving portions over a period of time, simply freeze individual slices. Freeze for around one month.
- Defrost in the refrigerator.

42. Thai Coconut Chicken

Servings 4

Ready in about 15 minutes

NUTRITIONAL INFORMATION (Per Serving)

192 - Calories
7.5g - Fat
5.4g - Carbs
25.2g - Protein
2.2g - Sugars

Ingredients

- 1 tablespoon coconut oil
- 1 pound chicken, cubed
- 1 shallot, peeled and chopped
- 2 cloves garlic, minced
- 1 teaspoon fresh ginger root, julienned
- 1/3 teaspoon cumin powder
- 1 teaspoon Thai chili, minced
- 1 cup vegetable broth, preferably homemade
- 1 tomato, peeled and chopped
- 1/3 cup coconut milk, unsweetened
- 1 teaspoon Thai curry paste
- 2 tablespoons tamari sauce
- 1/2 cup sprouts
- Salt and freshly ground black pepper, to taste

Directions

1. Press the "Sauté" button to heat up the Instant Pot. Now, heat the coconut oil. Cook the chicken for 2 to 3 minutes, stirring frequently; reserve.
2. Then, in pan drippings, cook the shallot and garlic until softened; add a splash of vegetable broth, if needed.
3. Add the ginger, cumin powder and Thai chili and cook until aromatic or 1 minute more.
4. Now, stir in the vegetable broth, tomato, coconut milk, Thai curry paste, and tamari sauce.
5. Secure the lid. Choose the "Manual" setting and cook for 10 minutes under High pressure. Once cooking is complete, use a quick pressure release; carefully remove the lid.
6. Afterwards, add the sprouts, salt, and black pepper. Let cool completely.

Storing

- Place the chicken in airtight containers or Ziploc bags; keep in your refrigerator for 3 to 4 days.
- For freezing, place the chicken in airtight containers or heavy-duty freezer bags. It will maintain the best quality for about 4 months. Defrost in the refrigerator. Enjoy!

43. Winter Chicken Salad

Servings 8

**Ready in about
15 minutes +
chilling time**

**NUTRITIONAL
INFORMATION
(Per Serving)**

343 - Calories
26.2g - Fat
1.6g - Carbs
24.9g - Protein
0.3g - Sugars

Ingredients

- 2 pounds chicken
- 1 cup vegetable broth
- 2 sprigs fresh thyme
- 1 teaspoon onion powder
- 1 teaspoon granulated garlic
- 1/2 teaspoon black pepper, ground
- 1 bay leaf
- 1 cup mayonnaise
- 1 teaspoon Dijon mustard
- 1 teaspoon fresh lemon juice
- 2 stalks celery, chopped
- 2 tablespoons fresh chives, chopped
- 1/2 teaspoon coarse sea salt

Directions

1. Place the chicken, broth, thyme, onion powder, garlic, black pepper, and bay leaf in your Instant Pot.
2. Secure the lid. Choose the "Poultry" setting and cook for 12 minutes under High pressure. Once cooking is complete, use a natural pressure release; carefully remove the lid.
3. Remove the chicken from the Instant Pot; allow it to cool slightly.
4. Now, cut the chicken breasts into strips and transfer it to a salad bowl. Add the remaining ingredients and gently stir until everything is well combined.

Storing

- Place the chicken salad in airtight containers or Ziploc bags; keep in your refrigerator for 3 to 5 days. Enjoy!

44. Italian-Style Turkey Meatloaf

Servings 6

Ready in about 35 minutes

NUTRITIONAL INFORMATION (Per Serving)

449 - Calories
29.7g - Fat
5.9g - Carbs
36.2g - Protein
2.7g - Sugars

Ingredients

- 2 pounds ground turkey
- 2/3 cup pork rind crumbs
- 1/2 cup Parmigiano-Reggiano, grated
- 1 tablespoon coconut aminos
- 2 eggs, chopped
- Sea salt, to taste
- 1/4 teaspoon ground black pepper
- 1 yellow onion, peeled and chopped
- 2 garlic cloves, minced
- 4 ounces tomato paste
- 1 tablespoon Italian seasoning
- 1/2 cup tomato sauce
- 1 cup water
- 1 teaspoon mustard powder
- 1/2 teaspoon chili powder

Directions

1. Prepare your Instant Pot by adding a metal rack and 1 ½ cups of water to the bottom of the inner pot.
2. In a large mixing bowl, thoroughly combine the ground turkey with pork rind crumbs, Parmigiano-Reggiano, coconut aminos, eggs, salt, black pepper, onion, garlic, tomato paste, Italian seasoning.
3. Shape this mixture into a meatloaf; lower your meatloaf onto the metal rack.
4. Then, in a mixing bowl, thoroughly combine the tomato sauce with water, mustard and chili powder. Spread this mixture over the top of your meatloaf.
5. Secure the lid. Choose the "Meat/Stew" setting and cook for 20 minutes at High pressure. Once cooking is complete, use a natural pressure release; carefully remove the lid.
6. Afterwards, place your meatloaf under the preheated broiler for 5 minutes. Allow the meatloaf to rest for 6 to 8 minutes before slicing and serving.

Storing

- Wrap the meatloaf tightly with heavy-duty aluminum foil or plastic wrap. Then, keep in your refrigerator for up to 3 to 4 days.
- For freezing, wrap the meatloaf tightly to prevent freezer burn. Freeze up to 3 to 4 months. Defrost in the refrigerator and reheat in your skillet. Bon appétit!

45. Family Pork Roast

Servings 6

Ready in about 30 minutes

NUTRITIONAL INFORMATION (Per Serving)

329 - Calories
18.2g - Fat
0g - Carbs
38.7g - Protein
0g - Sugars

Ingredients

- 2 teaspoons peanut oil
- 2 pounds pork tenderloin
- 1 cup beef bone broth
- 2 bay leaves
- 1 teaspoon mixed peppercorns

Directions

1. Massage the peanut oil into the pork.
2. Press the "Sauté" button to heat up the Instant Pot. Heat the oil and sear the meat for 2 to 3 minute on both sides.
3. Add the broth, bay leaves and mixed peppercorns to the Instant Pot.
4. Secure the lid. Choose the "Meat/Stew" setting and cook for 20 minutes under High pressure. Once cooking is complete, use a natural pressure release; carefully remove the lid. Let cool completely.

Storing

- Divide the pork between several airtight containers; keep in your refrigerator for 3 to 5 days.
- For freezing, place the pork in airtight containers or heavy-duty freezer bags. Freeze up to 2 to 3 months. Defrost in the refrigerator.

46. Za'atar-Rubbed Pork Shank

Servings 6

Ready in about 45 minutes

NUTRITIONAL INFORMATION (Per Serving)

328 - Calories
18.1g - Fat
6g - Carbs
30.6g - Protein
2.6g - Sugars

Ingredients

- 1 ½ pounds pork shank
- Seasoned salt and ground black pepper, to taste
- 2 tablespoons za'atar
- 1 tablespoon olive oil
- 1 medium-sized leek, sliced
- 2 garlic cloves, smashed
- 1 carrot, chopped
- 1 parsnip, chopped
- 1 celery with leaves, chopped
- 1 tablespoon dark soy sauce
- 1/2 teaspoon mustard powder
- 1 cup beef bone broth
- 1 tablespoon flaxseed meal

Directions

1. Generously season the pork shank with salt and black pepper. Now, sprinkle with za'atar on all sides.
2. Press the "Sauté" button to heat up the Instant Pot. Heat the olive oil. Once hot, sear the pork shank for 2 to 4 minute per side; reserve.
3. Now, sauté the leeks in pan drippings for 3 minutes.
4. After that, add the garlic, carrot parsnip, celery with leaves, soy sauce, mustard powder, and broth.
5. Add the pork shank back to the Instant Pot.
6. Secure the lid. Choose the "Meat/Stew" setting and cook for 35 minutes under High pressure. Once cooking is complete, use a natural pressure release; carefully remove the lid.
7. Mix the flaxseed meal with 1 tablespoon of water. Add this slurry to the Instant Pot. Press the "Sauté" button again to thicken the cooking liquid. Let cool completely.

Storing

- Place the pork shanks in airtight containers or Ziploc bags; keep in your refrigerator for up to 3 to 5 days.
- For freezing, place the pork shanks in airtight containers or heavy-duty freezer bags. Freeze up to 2 to 3 months. Defrost in the refrigerator. Bon appétit!

47. Zucchini Keto Lasagna

Servings 6

Ready in about 45 minutes

NUTRITIONAL INFORMATION (Per Serving)

533 - Calories
42.2g - Fat
6.1g - Carbs
32.6g - Protein
2.6g - Sugars

Ingredients

- 1 ½ pounds ground chuck
- 1/3 pound bacon, chopped
- 2 tablespoons yellow onion, chopped
- 2 cloves garlic, minced
- 4 eggs
- 8 ounces puréed tomatoes
- 1/2 cup double cream
- 1/2 cup ricotta cheese
- Sea salt and ground pepper, to your liking
- 1 teaspoon cayenne pepper
- 1/2 teaspoon celery seeds
- 1 teaspoon dried parsley flakes
- 10 ounces Monterey-Jack cheese, shredded
- 1 large zucchini, thinly sliced

Directions

1. Press the "Sauté" button to heat up the Instant Pot. Then, brown the meat and sausage for 2 to 3 minutes, crumbling it with a fork.
2. Add the onion and garlic; continue sautéing for 2 minutes more or until they are fragrant.
3. In a mixing bowl, thoroughly combine the eggs, puréed tomatoes, heavy cream, ricotta, salt, black pepper, cayenne pepper, celery seeds, and dried parsley.
4. Fold in 5 ounces of Monterey-Jack cheese and gently stir to combine.
5. In a casserole dish, place a layer of the ground meat. Then, create 2 layers of the zucchini crisscrossing.
6. Add a layer of the egg/cream mixture. Top with the remaining 5 ounces of shredded Monterey-Jack cheese.
7. Secure the lid. Choose "Meat/Stew" mode and High pressure; cook for 35 minutes. Once cooking is complete, use a quick pressure release; carefully remove the lid.
8. Let cool completely.

Storing

- Slice your lasagna into six pieces. Divide the pieces between airtight containers; it will last for 3 to 5 days in the refrigerator.
- For freezing, place each portion in a separate heavy-duty freezer bag. Freeze up to 2 to 3 months. Defrost in the microwave or refrigerator. Bon appétit!

48. Chili Hot Dog Bake

Servings 6

Ready in about 55 minutes

NUTRITIONAL INFORMATION (Per Serving)

452 - Calories
30.5g - Fat
5.8g - Carbs
35.6g - Protein
2.2g - Sugars

Ingredients

- 1 tablespoon olive oil
- 1 ½ pounds beef chuck, ground for chili
- Salt and ground black pepper, to taste
- 2 ripe tomatoes, chopped
- 1 onion, chopped
- 2 ounces tomato sauce
- 2 garlic cloves, pressed
- 1 chili pepper, minced
- 1 teaspoon smoked paprika
- 1/2 cup lager-style beer
- 1/2 cup water
- 6 beef hot dogs, sliced lengthwise
- 1 ½ cups Mexican cheese blend, shredded

Directions

1. Press the "Sauté" button to heat up the Instant Pot. Heat the olive oil and cook the beef until no longer pink. Season with salt and black pepper to taste.
2. Transfer the beef to a mixing dish. Then, add the tomatoes, onion, tomato sauce, garlic, chili pepper, and smoked paprika to the mixing dish.
3. Lay the hot dogs flat on the bottom of a lightly greased baking dish. Cover with the chili mixture. Pour in the beer and water.
4. Wipe down the Instant Pot with a damp cloth. Add 1 ½ cups of water and a metal rack to the Instant Pot.
5. Lower the baking dish onto the metal rack.
6. Secure the lid. Choose "Meat/Stew" mode and High pressure; cook for 35 minutes. Once cooking is complete, use a quick pressure release; carefully remove the lid.
7. Top with the shredded cheese and seal the lid. Let it sit for 5 minutes or until the cheese is completely melted.
8. Let cool completely.

Storing

- Slice it into six pieces. Divide the pieces between airtight containers; it will last for 3 to 5 days in the refrigerator.
- For freezing, place each portion in a separate heavy-duty freezer bag. Freeze up to 2 to 3 months. Defrost in the microwave or refrigerator. Bon appétit!

49. Herbed Cod Steaks

Servings 4

Ingredients

- 4 cod steaks, 1 ½-inch thick
- 2 tablespoons garlic-infused oil
- Sea salt, to taste
- 1/2 teaspoon mixed peppercorns, crushed
- 1 sprig rosemary
- 2 sprigs thyme
- 1 yellow onion, sliced

Ready in about 10 minutes

Directions

1. Prepare your Instant Pot by adding 1 ½ cups of water and a metal rack to the inner pot.
2. Then, massage the garlic-infused oil into the cod steaks; sprinkle them with salt and crushed peppercorns.
3. Lower the cod steaks onto the rack skin side down; place the rosemary, thyme, and onion on the top.
4. Secure the lid. Choose "Manual" mode and High pressure; cook for 4 minutes. Once cooking is complete, use a quick pressure release; carefully remove the lid.
5. Let cool completely.

NUTRITIONAL INFORMATION (Per Serving)

190 - Calories
7.7g - Fat
2.6g - Carbs
26.2g - Protein
1.1g - Sugars

Storing

- Place the cod steaks in airtight containers; they will last for 3 to 4 days in the refrigerator.
- For freezing, place the cod steaks in airtight containers or heavy-duty freezer bags. Freeze up to 2 to 3 months. Defrost in the refrigerator. Bon appétit!

50. Malabar Fish Curry

Servings 4

**Ready in about
15 minutes**

**NUTRITIONAL
INFORMATION
(Per Serving)**

235 - Calories
13.8g - Fat
5.8g - Carbs
19.5g - Protein
3.8g - Sugars

Ingredients

- 1 tablespoon canola oil
- 1/2 cup Cheriya ulli, finely sliced
- 1 red bell pepper, chopped
- 1 serrano pepper, chopped
- 1 teaspoon garlic, pressed
- 1 (1-inch) piece fresh ginger root, grated
- 4-5 curry leaves
- 1 pound Ocean perch, cut into bite-size pieces
- 1 teaspoon tamarind paste
- 2 tablespoons curry paste
- 2 ripe tomatoes, chopped
- 1/2 cup unsweetened coconut milk
- 1 ½ cup broth, preferably homemade
- Salt and ground black pepper, to taste

Directions

1. Press the "Sauté" button to heat up the Instant Pot. Now, heat the oil and sauté the Cheriya ulli and peppers until softened and fragrant.
2. Then, stir in the garlic, ginger, and curry leaves. Continue to sauté an additional minute or until they are fragrant.
3. Deglaze the bottom with the broth and add the remaining ingredients.
4. Secure the lid. Choose "Manual" mode and Low pressure; cook for 6 minutes. Once cooking is complete, use a quick pressure release; carefully remove the lid.
5. Taste and adjust the seasonings.
6. Let cool completely.

Storing

- Spoon the fish curry into airtight containers; it will last for 3 to 4 days in the refrigerator.
- For freezing, place the fish curry in airtight containers or heavy-duty freezer bags. Freeze up to 4 to 6 months. Defrost in the microwave or refrigerator. Bon appétit!

51. Basil Wine Scallops

Servings 5

Ready in about 10 minutes

NUTRITIONAL
INFORMATION
(Per Serving)

209 - Calories
10.5g - Fat
5.7g - Carbs
19.2g - Protein
2.6g - Sugars

Ingredients

- 1 tablespoon olive oil
- 1 brown onion, chopped
- 2 garlic cloves, minced
- 1/2 cup port wine
- 1 ½ pounds scallops, peeled and deveined
- 1/2 cup fish stock
- 1 ripe tomato, crushed
- Sea salt and ground black pepper, to taste
- 1 teaspoon smoked paprika
- 2 tablespoons fresh lemon juice
- 1/2 cup cream cheese, at room temperature
- 2 tablespoons fresh basil, chopped

Directions

1. Press the "Sauté" button to heat up your Instant Pot. Now, heat the oil and cook the onion and garlic until fragrant.
2. Add the wine to deglaze the bottom. Add the scallops, fish stock, tomato, salt, black pepper, and paprika.
3. Secure the lid. Choose "Manual" mode and Low pressure; cook for 1 minute. Once cooking is complete, use a quick pressure release; carefully remove the lid.
4. Drizzle fresh lemon juice over the scallops and top them with cream cheese. Cover and let it sit in the residual heat for 3 to 5 minutes. Garnish with fresh basil leaves. Let cool completely.

Storing

- Spoon the cooked scallops into an airtight container; keep in your refrigerator for 3 to 4 days.
- For freezing, place the cooked scallops in airtight containers or heavy-duty freezer bags. Freeze up to 3 months. Defrost in the microwave. Bon appétit!

52. Simple Garlicky Halibut Steak

Servings 3

Ready in about 10 minutes

NUTRITIONAL INFORMATION
(Per Serving)

287 - Calories
20.9g - Fat
1.3g - Carbs
21.9g - Protein
0g - Sugars

Ingredients

- 3 halibut steaks
- 4 garlic cloves, crushed
- Coarse sea salt, to taste
- 1/4 teaspoon ground black pepper, to taste

Directions

1. Prepare your Instant Pot by adding 1 ½ cups of water and steamer basket to the inner pot.
2. Place the halibut steaks in the steamer basket; season them with salt and black pepper.
3. Secure the lid. Choose "Manual" mode and High pressure; cook for 5 minutes. Once cooking is complete, use a quick pressure release; carefully remove the lid. Let cool completely.

Storing

- Place the halibut steaks in airtight containers; they will last for 3 to 4 days in the refrigerator.
- For freezing, place the halibut steaks in airtight containers or heavy-duty freezer bags. Freeze up to 2 to 3 months. Defrost in the refrigerator. Bon appétit!

53. Vegetables à la Grecque

Servings 4

Ready in about 20 minutes

NUTRITIONAL
INFORMATION
(Per Serving)

326 - Calories
25.1g - Fat
4.9g - Carbs
15.7g - Protein
4.3g - Sugars

Ingredients

- 2 tablespoons olive oil
- 2 garlic cloves, minced
- 1 red onion, chopped
- 10 ounces button mushrooms, thinly sliced
- 1 (1-pound) eggplant, sliced
- 1/2 teaspoon dried basil
- 1 teaspoon dried oregano
- 1 thyme sprig, leaves picked
- 2 rosemary sprigs, leaves picked
- 1/2 cup tomato sauce
- 1/4 cup dry Greek wine
- 1/4 cup water
- 8 ounces Halloumi cheese, cubed
- 4 tablespoons Kalamata olives, pitted and halved

Directions

1. Press the "Sauté" button to heat up your Instant Pot; now, heat the olive oil. Cook the garlic and red onions for 1 to 2 minutes, stirring periodically.
2. Stir in the mushrooms and continue to sauté an additional 2 to 3 minutes.
3. Add the eggplant, basil, oregano, thyme, rosemary, tomato sauce, Greek wine, and water.
4. Secure the lid. Choose "Manual" mode and Low pressure; cook for 3 minutes. Once cooking is complete, use a quick pressure release; carefully remove the lid.
5. Top with cheese and olives. Let cool completely.

Storing

- Divide the vegetables into four portions; divide the portions between four airtight containers; keep in your refrigerator for up 3 to 5 days.
- For freezing, wrap them tightly with plastic wrap and place in airtight containers. Freeze up to 10 to 12 months. Defrost in the refrigerator. Bon appétit!

54. Turnip Greens with Sausage

Servings 4

Ready in about 10 minutes

Ingredients

- 2 teaspoons sesame oil
- 2 pork sausages, casing removed sliced
- 2 garlic cloves, minced
- 1 medium-sized leek, chopped
- 1 pound turnip greens
- 1 cup turkey bone stock
- Sea salt, to taste
- 1/4 teaspoon ground black pepper, or more to taste
- 1 bay leaf
- 1 tablespoon black sesame seeds

Directions

1. Press the "Sauté" button to heat up the Instant Pot. Then, heat the sesame oil; cook the sausage until nice and delicately browned; set aside.
2. Add the garlic and leeks; continue to cook in pan drippings for a minute or two.
3. Add the greens, stock, salt, black pepper, and bay leaf.
4. Secure the lid. Choose "Manual" mode and Low pressure; cook for 3 minutes. Once cooking is complete, use a quick pressure release; carefully remove the lid.
5. Add the black sesame seeds. Let cool completely.

NUTRITIONAL INFORMATION (Per Serving)

149 - Calories
7.2g - Fat
9g - Carbs
14.2g - Protein
2.2g - Sugars

Storing

- Place the mixture in an airtight container; place in the refrigerator for 3 to 4 days.
- To freeze, place in Ziploc bags and freeze up to 3 months. To defrost, place in your microwave for a few minutes.

55. Indian-Style Cauliflower

Servings 4

Ready in about 10 minutes

NUTRITIONAL INFORMATION (Per Serving)

101 - Calories
7.2g - Fat
6.6g - Carbs
2.3g - Protein
3.6g - Sugars

Ingredients

- 2 tablespoons grapeseed oil
- 1/2 cup scallions, chopped
- 2 cloves garlic, pressed
- 1 tablespoon garam masala
- 1 teaspoon curry powder
- 1 red chili pepper, minced
- 1/2 teaspoon ground cumin
- Sea salt and ground black pepper, to taste
- 1 tablespoon fresh coriander, chopped
- 1 teaspoon ajwain
- 2 tomatoes, puréed
- 1 pound cauliflower, broken into florets
- 1/2 cup water
- 1/2 cup almond yogurt

Directions

1. Press the "Sauté" button to heat up your Instant Pot. Now, heat the oil and sauté the scallions for 1 minute.
2. Add the garlic and continue to cook an additional 30 seconds or until aromatic.
3. Add the garam masala, curry powder, chili pepper, cumin, salt, black pepper, coriander, ajwain, tomatoes, cauliflower, and water.
4. Secure the lid. Choose "Manual" mode and High pressure; cook for 3 minutes. Once cooking is complete, use a quick pressure release; carefully remove the lid.
5. Pour in the almond yogurt and stir well. Let cool completely.

Storing

- Place the cauliflower in airtight containers; keep in your refrigerator for 3 to 5 days.
- Place the cauliflower in freezable containers; they will maintain the best quality for 10 to 12 months. Defrost in the refrigerator or microwave. Enjoy!

56. Green Beans with Scallions and Mushrooms

Servings 4

Ready in about 10 minutes

NUTRITIONAL INFORMATION (Per Serving)

106 - Calories
7.7g - Fat
6g - Carbs
3.5g - Protein
1.7g - Sugars

Ingredients

- 2 tablespoons olive oil
- 1/2 cup scallions, chopped
- 2 cloves garlic, minced
- 1 cup white mushrooms, chopped
- 3/4 pound green beans
- 1 cup vegetable broth
- Sea salt and ground black pepper, to taste
- 1 teaspoon red pepper flakes, crushed

Directions

1. Press the "Sauté" button to heat up your Instant Pot. Heat the oil and sauté scallions until softened or about 2 minutes.
2. Then, add the garlic and mushrooms; continue to cook an additional minute or so.
3. Add the other ingredients; gently stir to combine.
4. Secure the lid. Choose "Manual" mode and Low pressure; cook for 3 minutes. Once cooking is complete, use a quick pressure release; carefully remove the lid.
5. Let cool completely.

Storing

- Place the green beans in airtight containers; keep in your refrigerator for 3 to 5 days.
- Place the green beans in freezable containers; they will maintain the best quality for 10 to 12 months. Defrost in the refrigerator or microwave. Enjoy!

57. Traditional Sunday Ratatouille

Servings 4

Ready in about 35 minutes

NUTRITIONAL INFORMATION (Per Serving)

102 - Calories
7.1g - Fat
6.4g - Carbs
1.7g - Protein
5.9g - Sugars

Ingredients

- 1 eggplant, peeled and sliced
- 2 teaspoons of table salt
- 2 tablespoons olive oil
- 1 purple onion, thinly sliced
- 3 garlic cloves, chopped
- 1 teaspoon hot paprika
- 1 red bell pepper, seeded and sliced
- 1 yellow bell pepper, seeded and sliced
- 2 large-sized tomatoes, chopped
- 1/4 teaspoon freshly ground black pepper
- 1/3 teaspoon cayenne pepper
- 1/3 teaspoon dried basil
- 1/4 teaspoon tarragon
- Sea salt, to taste

Directions

1. Place the eggplant cubes with 2 teaspoons of table salt in a ceramic dish. Let it sit for 25 to 30 minutes. Drain and rinse the eggplant.
2. Press the "Sauté" button to heat up your Instant Pot. Heat the oil and sauté the eggplant until tender.
3. Add the remaining ingredients and gently stir to combine.
4. Secure the lid. Choose "Manual" mode and High pressure; cook for 3 minutes. Once cooking is complete, use a quick pressure release; carefully remove the lid.
5. Let cool completely.

Storing

- Place the Ratatouille in airtight containers; keep in your refrigerator for 3 to 5 days.
- Place the Ratatouille in freezable containers; it will maintain the best quality for 10 to 12 months. Defrost in the refrigerator or microwave. Enjoy!

58. Kid-Friendly Mini Frittatas

Servings 4

**Ready in about
15 minutes**

**NUTRITIONAL
INFORMATION
(Per Serving)**

314 - Calories
25.6g - Fat
2.9g - Carbs
16.7g - Protein
1.7g - Sugars

Ingredients

- **4 eggs**
- **1/4 cup full-fat milk**
- **Sea salt, to taste**
- **1/4 teaspoon ground black pepper**
- **1/4 teaspoon cayenne pepper, or more to taste**
- **1/2 teaspoon granulated garlic**
- **1/3 teaspoon ground bay leaf**
- **1/2 teaspoon dried dill weed**
- **1 cup Chorizo sausage, chopped**
- **1/2 cup green onions, chopped**

Directions

1. Prepare your Instant Pot by adding 1 cup of water and a metal trivet to the bottom of the inner pot.
2. Thoroughly combine all ingredients until everything is well mixed. Spoon the mixture into silicone molds.
3. Lower the silicone molds onto the trivet.
4. Secure the lid. Choose "Manual" mode and High pressure; cook for 7 minutes. Once cooking is complete, use a quick pressure release; carefully remove the lid. Let cool completely.

Storing

- Place the mini frittatas in the airtight containers or Ziploc bags; keep in the refrigerator for a week.
- For freezing, divide the mini frittatas among Ziploc bags and freeze up to 3 months. Defrost in your microwave for a couple of minutes. Bon appétit!

59. Hot Lager Chicken Wings

Servings 6

Ready in about 15 minutes

NUTRITIONAL INFORMATION (Per Serving)

216 - Calories
16.4g - Fat
2.2g - Carbs
12.9g - Protein
0.5g - Sugars

Ingredients

- 2 tablespoons butter, melted
- 1 pound chicken thighs
- Coarse sea salt and ground black pepper, to taste
- 1 teaspoon cayenne pepper
- 1 teaspoon shallot powder
- 1 teaspoon garlic powder
- 1 teaspoon hot sauce
- 1/2 cup lager
- 1/2 cup water

Directions

1. Press the "Sauté" button and melt the butter. Once hot, brown the chicken thighs for 2 minutes per side.
2. Add the remaining ingredients to your Instant Pot.
3. Secure the lid. Choose "Poultry" mode and High pressure; cook for 6 minutes. Once cooking is complete, use a quick pressure release; carefully remove the lid.
4. Let cool completely.

Storing

- Place the chicken wings in airtight containers or Ziploc bags; keep in your refrigerator for up 3 to 4 days.
- For freezing, place the chicken wings in airtight containers or heavy-duty freezer bags. Freeze up to 3 months. Once thawed in the refrigerator, heat in the preheated oven at 375 degrees F for 20 to 25 minutes or until heated through.

60. Beef Short Ribs with Cilantro Cream

Servings 8

Ready in about 25 minutes

NUTRITIONAL INFORMATION (Per Serving)

346 - Calories
24.1g - Fat
2.1g - Carbs
31g - Protein
1.1g - Sugars

Ingredients

- 1 tablespoon sesame oil
- 2 ½ pounds beef short ribs
- 1/2 teaspoon red pepper flakes, crushed
- Sea salt and ground black pepper, to taste

- **Cilantro Cream:**
- 1 cup cream cheese, softened
- 1/3 cup sour cream
- A pinch of celery salt
- A pinch of paprika
- 1 teaspoon garlic powder
- 1 bunch fresh cilantro, chopped
- 1 tablespoon fresh lime juice

Directions

1. Press the "Sauté" button to heat up the Instant Pot. Now, heat the sesame oil. Sear the ribs until nicely browned on all sides.
2. Season the ribs with red pepper, salt, and black pepper.
3. Secure the lid. Choose "Manual" mode and High pressure; cook for 20 minutes. Once cooking is complete, use a quick pressure release; carefully remove the lid.
4. Meanwhile, mix all ingredients for the cilantro cream. Let cool completely.

Storing

- Divide the beef short ribs into eight portions. Place each portion of ribs in an airtight container; keep in your refrigerator for 3 to 5 days.
- For freezing, place the ribs in airtight containers or heavy-duty freezer bags. Freeze up to 4 to 6 months. Defrost in the refrigerator. Reheat in your oven at 250 degrees F until heated through.
- Place the Cilantro Cream in an airtight container; keep in your refrigerator for 1 week.
- For freezing, place the Cilantro Cream in an airtight container or a heavy-duty freezer bag; it will maintain the best quality for about 2 months. Bon appétit!

VEGAN

61. Aromatic Garlicky Zucchini

Servings 4

Ingredients

- 1 ½ tablespoons olive oil
- 2 garlic cloves, minced
- 1 ½ pounds zucchinis, sliced
- 1/2 cup vegetable broth
- Salt and pepper, to taste
- 1/2 teaspoon dried rosemary
- 1 teaspoon dried basil
- 1/2 teaspoon smoked paprika

Ready in about 10 minutes

Directions

1. Press the "Sauté" button to heat up your Instant Pot. Now, heat the olive oil and cook the garlic until aromatic.
2. Add the remaining ingredients.
3. Secure the lid. Choose "Manual" mode and Low pressure; cook for 3 minutes. Once cooking is complete, use a quick pressure release; carefully remove the lid. Let cool completely.

**NUTRITIONAL
INFORMATION
(Per Serving)**

88 - Calories
5.9g - Fat
5.1g - Carbs
5.3g - Protein
0.1g - Sugars

Storing

- Place the zucchini in airtight containers or Ziploc bags; keep in your refrigerator for 3 to 5 days.
- Place the zucchini in a freezable container; they can be frozen for up to 10 to 12 months. Bake the thawed zucchini at 200 degrees F until they are completely warm. Enjoy!

62. Creamed Asparagus and Mushroom Soup

Servings 4

Ready in about 15 minutes

NUTRITIONAL INFORMATION (Per Serving)

171 - Calories
11.7g- Fat
7.2g - Carbs
9.7g - Protein
3.4g - Sugars

Ingredients

- 2 tablespoons coconut oil
- 1/2 cup shallots, chopped
- 2 cloves garlic, minced
- 1 pound asparagus, washed, trimmed and chopped
- 4 ounces button mushrooms, sliced
- 4 cups vegetable broth
- 2 tablespoons balsamic vinegar
- Himalayan salt, to taste
- 1/4 teaspoon ground black pepper
- 1/4 teaspoon paprika

Directions

1. Press the "Sauté" button to heat up your Instant Pot. Heat the oil and cook the shallots and garlic for 2 to 3 minutes.
2. Add the remaining ingredients to the Instant Pot.
3. Secure the lid. Choose "Manual" mode and High pressure; cook for 4 minutes. Once cooking is complete, use a quick pressure release; carefully remove the lid.
4. Let cool completely.

Storing

- Spoon the soup into airtight containers; keep in your refrigerator for up 3 to 4 days.
- For freezing, place the soup in airtight containers or heavy-duty freezer bags. Freeze up to 4 to 6 months. Defrost in the microwave or refrigerator. Enjoy!

63. Asian-Style Vegan Stew

Servings 4

Ready in about 20 minutes

NUTRITIONAL INFORMATION (Per Serving)

136 - Calories
7.3g - Fat
6.3g - Carbs
2.6g - Protein
3.5g - Sugars

Ingredients

- 2 tablespoons sesame oil
- 1 red onion, chopped
- 1 teaspoon ginger-garlic paste
- 1 celery stalk, sliced
- 1 carrot, sliced
- 3 cups brown mushrooms, sliced
- 2 ripe Roma tomatoes, puréed
- 1 cup vegetable broth, preferably homemade
- 1 (12-ounce) bottle amber beer
- 2 bay leaves
- 1/2 teaspoon caraway seeds
- 1/4 teaspoon cumin seeds
- 1/2 teaspoon fenugreek seeds
- Sea salt and ground black pepper, to taste
- 1 teaspoon Hungarian hot paprika
- 1 tablespoon soy sauce

Directions

1. Press the "Sauté" button to heat up your Instant Pot. Heat the sesame oil and cook the onions for 2 to 3 minutes or until tender and translucent.
2. Now, add the ginger-garlic paste, celery, carrot and mushrooms; continue to cook for a further 2 minutes or until fragrant.
3. Add the remaining ingredients, except for the soy sauce.
4. Secure the lid. Choose "Manual" mode and High pressure; cook for 10 minutes. Once cooking is complete, use a quick pressure release; carefully remove the lid.
5. Add a few drizzles of soy sauce to the soup. Let cool completely.

Storing

- Spoon your stew into airtight containers; keep in your refrigerator for up 3 to 4 days.
- For freezing, place it in airtight containers or heavy-duty freezer bags. Freeze up to 4 to 6 months. Defrost in the microwave or refrigerator. Enjoy!

64. Easy Chunky Autumn Soup

Servings 4

Ready in about 10 minutes

NUTRITIONAL
INFORMATION
(Per Serving)

99 - Calories
5.5g - Fat
7.1g - Carbs
2g - Protein
3.4g - Sugars

Ingredients

- 1 ½ tablespoons olive oil
- 1 leek, chopped
- 2 cloves garlic, smashed
- 1 parsnip, chopped
- 1 celery stalk, chopped
- 4 cups water
- 2 bouillon cubes
- 1/2 pound green cabbage, shredded
- 1 zucchini, sliced
- 2 bay leaves
- 1/2 teaspoon ground cumin
- 1/2 teaspoon turmeric powder
- 1 teaspoon dried basil
- Kosher salt and ground black pepper, to taste
- 6 ounces Swiss chard

Directions

1. Press the "Sauté" button to heat up your Instant Pot. Heat the olive oil and cook the leek for 2 to 3 minutes or until it is softened.
2. Add the other ingredients, except for the Swiss chard, to the Instant Pot; stir to combine well.
3. Secure the lid. Choose "Manual" mode and High pressure; cook for 3 minutes. Once cooking is complete, use a quick pressure release; carefully remove the lid.
4. Add the Swiss chard and cover with the lid. Allow it to sit in the residual heat until it is wilted.
5. Discard the bay leaves. Let cool completely.

Storing

- Spoon the soup into airtight containers or Ziploc bags; keep in your refrigerator for up to 3 to 4 days.
- For freezing, place the soup in airtight containers. It will maintain the best quality for about 4 to 6 months. Defrost in the refrigerator. Bon appétit!

65. Party Cauliflower Balls

Servings 8

Ready in about 15 minutes

NUTRITIONAL INFORMATION (Per Serving)

60 - Calories
4.8g - Fat
4g - Carbs
1.5g - Protein
1.1g - Sugars

Ingredients

- 1 pound cauliflower, broken into florets
- 2 teaspoons vegan margarine
- 1/3 cup coconut cream
- Sea salt, to taste
- 1/3 teaspoon ground black pepper
- A pinch of freshly grated nutmeg
- 2 cloves garlic, peeled
- 3 tablespoons Kalamata olives, pitted
- 2 tablespoons smoked paprika

Directions

1. Add 1 cup of water and a steamer basket to the bottom of your Instant Pot.
2. Then, arrange the cauliflower and kohlrabi in the steamer basket.
3. Secure the lid. Choose "Manual" mode and High pressure; cook for 2 minutes. Once cooking is complete, use a quick pressure release; carefully remove the lid.
4. Purée your cauliflower along with the remaining ingredients in a food processor.
5. Form the mixture into balls and roll each ball into smoked the paprika powder. Let cool completely.

Storing

- Transfer the balls to the airtight containers and place in your refrigerator for up to 3 to 4 days.
- For freezing, place the balls in freezer safe containers and freeze up to 1 month. Defrost in the microwave for a few minutes.

66. Croatian Blitva with Dry Sherry

Servings 4

**Ready in about
5 minutes**

NUTRITIONAL
INFORMATION
(Per Serving)

109 - Calories
7.1g - Fat
6g - Carbs
2.8g - Protein
2.8g - Sugars

Ingredients

- 2 tablespoons olive oil
- 1 teaspoon garlic, minced
- 1 cup scallions, chopped
- 1 ripe tomato, puréed
- 1 pound Swiss chard, torn into pieces
- 1/4 cup dry sherry
- 2 tablespoons dried parsley
- 1/4 teaspoon basil

Directions

1. Press the "Sauté" button to heat up your Instant Pot. Heat the oil and sauté the garlic approximately 40 seconds or until aromatic.
2. Add the remaining ingredients and stir to combine well.
3. Secure the lid. Choose "Manual" mode and Low pressure; cook for 2 minutes. Once cooking is complete, use a quick pressure release; carefully remove the lid.
4. Let cool completely.

Storing

- Place the Swiss chard in airtight containers or Ziploc bags; keep in your refrigerator for up to 3 to 5 days.
- For freezing, place the Swiss chard in airtight containers or heavy-duty freezer bags. Freeze up to 10 months. Defrost in the refrigerator. Bon appétit!

67. Sriracha Carrot and Chard Purée

Servings 4

Ready in about 15 minutes

NUTRITIONAL INFORMATION (Per Serving)

140 - Calories
11.3g - Fat
7.1g - Carbs
2.3g - Protein
4.4g - Sugars

Ingredients

- 2 cups carrots, peeled and chopped
- 10 ounces fresh or frozen (and thawed) chard, torn into pieces
- Sea salt, to taste
- 1/4 teaspoon ground black pepper, to taste
- 1/2 teaspoon garlic powder
- 1/2 teaspoon shallot power
- 1/2 teaspoon fennel seeds
- 1 teaspoon cayenne pepper
- 1 teaspoon Sriracha chili sauce
- 2 tablespoons coconut oil
- 3/4 cup vegetable broth
- 1/3 cup coconut cream

Directions

1. Add all ingredients, except for the coconut cream, to your Instant Pot.
2. Secure the lid. Choose "Manual" mode and High pressure; cook for 2 minutes. Once cooking is complete, use a quick pressure release; carefully remove the lid.
3. Transfer the vegetable mixture to your food processor; add the coconut cream and purée the mixture until uniform, creamy, and smooth. Let cool completely.

Storing

- Place the chilled puree in airtight containers or Ziploc bags; keep in your refrigerator for up to 3 to 5 days.
- To freeze, place the chilled puree in storage bags. Freeze for about 10 to 12 months. Bon appétit!

68. Broccoli Bake with Vegan Béchamel

Servings 4

Ready in about 20 minutes

NUTRITIONAL INFORMATION (Per Serving)

130 - Calories
7.9g - Fat
6.5g - Carbs
8.4g - Protein
3.1g - Sugars

Ingredients

- 1/2 cup sunflower seeds, soaked overnight
- 2 tablespoons sesame seeds
- 1 cup water
- 1 cup almond milk, unsweetened
- 1/4 teaspoon grated nutmeg
- 1/2 teaspoon sea salt
- 1 tablespoon nutritional yeast
- 2 tablespoons rice vinegar
- 1 pound broccoli, broken into florets
- 1/2 cup spring onions, chopped
- 10 ounces white fresh mushrooms, sliced
- Sea salt and white pepper, to taste
- 1 tablespoon cayenne pepper
- 1/4 teaspoon dried dill
- 1/4 teaspoon bay leaf, ground

Directions

1. Add the sunflower seeds, sesame seeds, water, milk, nutmeg, 1/2 teaspoon of sea salt, nutritional yeast, and vinegar to your blender.
2. Blend until smooth and uniform.
3. Spritz a casserole dish with a nonstick cooking spray. Add the broccoli, spring onions and mushrooms.
4. Sprinkle with salt, white pepper, cayenne pepper, dill, and ground bay leaf. Pour the prepared vegan béchamel over your casserole.
5. Add 1 cup of water and a metal rack to your Instant Pot. Place the dish on the rack.
6. Secure the lid. Choose "Manual" mode and High pressure; cook for 3 minutes. Once cooking is complete, use a quick pressure release; carefully remove the lid.
7. Let cool completely.

Storing

- Cut the Broccoli Bake into four pieces. Place each piece in a separate airtight container or Ziploc bag; keep for 3 to 4 days in the refrigerator.
- To freeze, place each piece in a separate heavy-duty freezer bag. Freeze up to 6 months. Defrost in the microwave or refrigerator. Bon appétit!

69. Everyday Italian Pepperonata

Servings 4

Ready in about 15 minutes

NUTRITIONAL INFORMATION (Per Serving)

308 - Calories
30.6g - Fat
5.9g - Carbs
5.6g - Protein
1.1g - Sugars

Ingredients

- 2 tablespoons grapeseed oil
- 1/2 cup onions, chopped
- 2 green bell peppers, seeded and chopped
- 1 red bell pepper, seeded and chopped
- 1 yellow bell pepper, seeded and chopped
- 1 red chili pepper, seeded and minced
- 2 tomatoes, pureed
- 2 garlic cloves, crushed
- 1 tablespoon balsamic vinegar
- 1 teaspoon dried basil
- 1 teaspoon dried oregano
- 1 teaspoon dried thyme
- 1/4 cup Italian dry white wine
- 3/4 cup vegetable broth
- Sea salt and ground black pepper, to taste
- 1 teaspoon paprika
- 2 tablespoons fresh Italian parsley, roughly chopped

Directions

1. Press the "Sauté" button to heat up your Instant Pot. Heat the oil and sauté the onion until it is softened.
2. Add the other ingredients, except for the Italian parsley.
3. Secure the lid. Choose "Manual" mode and High pressure; cook for 3 minutes. Once cooking is complete, use a quick pressure release; carefully remove the lid.
4. Press the "Sauté" button again to thicken the cooking liquid; let it simmer for 3 to 4 minutes.
5. Garnish with fresh parsley. Let cool completely.

Storing

- Place the Italian Pepperonata in airtight containers; keep in your refrigerator for 3 to 5 days.
- Place the Italian Pepperonata in freezable containers; it will maintain the best quality for 10 to 12 months. Defrost in the refrigerator or microwave. Enjoy!

70. Summer Veggie Kabobs

Servings 5

Ready in about
10 minutes

NUTRITIONAL
INFORMATION
(Per Serving)

126 - Calories
9.5g - Fat
6.1g - Carbs
3.7g - Protein
2.4g - Sugars

Ingredients

- 1/2 head of broccoli, broken into florets
- 1/2 head of cauliflower, broken into florets
- 1 red bell pepper, seeded and diced
- 1 green bell pepper, seeded and diced
- 1 orange bell pepper, seeded and diced
- 9 ounces button mushrooms
- 2 cups cherry tomatoes
- 1 teaspoon ground coriander
- 1 teaspoon cayenne pepper
- Coarse sea salt and ground black pepper, to taste
- 1/4 cup olive oil

Directions

1. Prepare your Instant Pot by adding 1 cup of water and a metal rack to its bottom.
2. Thread your broccoli, cauliflower, bell peppers, mushrooms, and cherry tomatoes onto small bamboo skewers.
3. Sprinkle them with the coriander, cayenne pepper, salt and black pepper. Drizzle with olive oil and transfer the skewers to the rack.
4. Secure the lid. Choose "Manual" mode and High pressure; cook for 3 minutes. Once cooking is complete, use a quick pressure release; carefully remove the lid.
5. Let cool completely.

Storing

- Place the vegetable skewers in airtight containers; keep in your refrigerator for 3 to 5 days.
- Place the vegetable skewers in freezable containers; it will maintain the best quality for 10 to 12 months. Defrost in the refrigerator or microwave. Enjoy!

71. Thai Cream of Celery Soup

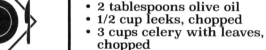

Servings 4

Ingredients

- 2 tablespoons olive oil
- 1/2 cup leeks, chopped
- 3 cups celery with leaves, chopped
- 2 cloves garlic, smashed
- 1 (2-inch) piece young galangal, peeled and chopped
- 1 teaspoon shallot powder
- 2 fresh bird chilies, seeded and finely chopped
- 4 cups water
- 2 tablespoons vegetable bouillon granules
- 1/2 teaspoon Thai white peppercorns, ground
- Sea salt, to taste
- 1 bay leaf
- 1/4 cup coconut cream, unsweetened
- 2 sprigs cilantro, coarsely chopped

Ready in about 10 minutes

Directions

1. Press the "Sauté" button to heat up your Instant Pot. Heat the oil and sauté the leeks until tender or about 2 minutes.
2. Add the celery, garlic, and galangal; continue to cook an additional 2 minutes.
3. Next, add the shallot powder, bird chilies, water, vegetable bouillon granules, Thai white peppercorns, salt, and bay leaf.
4. Secure the lid. Choose "Manual" mode and High pressure; cook for 2 minutes. Once cooking is complete, use a quick pressure release; carefully remove the lid.
5. Afterwards, purée the soup with an immersion blender until smooth and uniform; then, return the soup to the Instant Pot.
6. Add the coconut cream and press the "Sauté" button again. Let it simmer until everything is heated through.
7. Garnish with cilantro. Let cool completely.

NUTRITIONAL INFORMATION (Per Serving)

141 - Calories
11.1g - Fat
6.9g - Carbs
2.2g - Protein
4.2g - Sugars

Storing

- Spoon the soup into airtight containers or Ziploc bags; keep in your refrigerator for up to 3 to 4 days.
- For freezing, place the soup in airtight containers. It will maintain the best quality for about 4 to 6 months. Defrost in the refrigerator. Bon appétit!

72. Zucchini and Leek Soup

Servings 4

**Ready in about
15 minutes**

**NUTRITIONAL
INFORMATION
(Per Serving)**

90 - Calories
7.4g - Fat
4.9g - Carbs
2g - Protein
1.5g - Sugars

Ingredients

- 2 tablespoons coconut oil
- 1 medium-sized leek, thinly sliced
- 1 zucchini, chopped
- 2 garlic cloves, crushed
- Sea salt and ground black pepper, to your liking
- 1/2 teaspoon cayenne pepper
- 4 cups vegetable stock
- 1/4 cup coriander leaves, chopped

Directions

1. Press the "Sauté" button to heat up your Instant Pot. Heat the coconut oil and sauté the leeks, zucchini, and garlic.
2. Next, stir in the salt, black pepper, cayenne pepper, and stock.
3. Secure the lid. Choose "Manual" mode and High pressure; cook for 8 minutes. Once cooking is complete, use a natural pressure release; carefully remove the lid.
4. Garnish with coriander leaves. Let cool completely.

Storing

- Spoon the soup into airtight containers or Ziploc bags; keep in your refrigerator for up to 3 to 4 days.
- For freezing, place the soup in airtight containers. It will maintain the best quality for about 4 to 6 months. Defrost in the refrigerator. Bon appétit!

73. Winter One-Pot-Wonder

Servings 4

Ready in about
15 minutes

NUTRITIONAL
INFORMATION
(Per Serving)

157 - Calories
12.3g - Fat
7.4g - Carbs
3.4g - Protein
4.7g - Sugars

Ingredients

- 10 ounces coconut milk
- 10 ounces vegetable stock
- 1 garlic cloves, minced
- 1 teaspoon fresh ginger root, grated
- 4 tablespoons almond butter
- Sea salt and ground black pepper, to taste
- 1/2 teaspoon turmeric powder
- A pinch of grated nutmeg
- 1/2 teaspoon ground coriander
- 10 ounces pumpkin, cubed
- 1/3 cup leek, white part only, finely sliced

Directions

1. Place the milk, stock, garlic, ginger, almond butter, salt, black pepper, turmeric powder, nutmeg, coriander, and pumpkin in your Instant Pot.
2. Secure the lid. Choose "Manual" mode and High pressure; cook for 10 minutes. Once cooking is complete, use a natural pressure release; carefully remove the lid.
3. Now, blend your soup with a stick blender. Add the finely sliced leeks.
4. Let cool completely.

Storing

- Spoon the soup into airtight containers or Ziploc bags; keep in your refrigerator for up to 3 to 4 days.
- For freezing, place the soup in airtight containers. It will maintain the best quality for about 4 to 6 months. Defrost in the refrigerator. Bon appétit!

74. Vegan Mushroom Stroganoff

Servings 4

Ready in about 10 minutes

NUTRITIONAL INFORMATION (Per Serving)

128 - Calories
9.1g - Fat
6.6g - Carbs
6g - Protein
3.7g - Sugars

Ingredients

- 2 tablespoons olive oil
- 1/2 teaspoon caraway seeds, crushed
- 1/2 cup onion, chopped
- 2 garlic cloves, smashed
- 1/4 cup vodka
- 3/4 pound button mushrooms, chopped
- 1 celery stalk, chopped
- 1 ripe tomato, puréed
- 1 teaspoon mustard seeds
- Sea salt and freshly ground pepper, to your liking
- 2 cups vegetable broth

Directions

1. Press the "Sauté" button to heat up your Instant Pot. Now, heat the oil and sauté the caraway seeds until fragrant, about 40 seconds.
2. Then, add the onion and garlic, and continue sautéing for 1 to 2 minutes more, stirring frequently.
3. After that, add the remaining ingredients and stir to combine.
4. Secure the lid. Choose "Manual" mode and High pressure; cook for 5 minutes. Once cooking is complete, use a quick pressure release; carefully remove the lid.
5. Let cool completely.

Storing

- Spoon your stew into airtight containers; keep in your refrigerator for up 3 to 5 days.
- For freezing, place it in airtight containers or heavy-duty freezer bags. Freeze up to 6 months. Defrost in the microwave or refrigerator. Enjoy!

FAST SNACKS & APPETIZERS

75. Easy Spinach Dip

Servings 10

**Ready in about
5 minutes**

**NUTRITIONAL
INFORMATION
(Per Serving)**

43 - Calories
1.7g - Fat
3.5g - Carbs
4.1g - Protein
1.3g - Sugars

Ingredients

- 1 pound spinach
- 4 ounces Cottage cheese, at room temperature
- 4 ounces Cheddar cheese, grated
- 1 teaspoon garlic powder
- 1/2 teaspoon shallot powder
- 1/2 teaspoon celery seeds
- 1/2 teaspoon fennel seeds
- 1/2 teaspoon cayenne pepper
- Salt and black pepper, to taste

Directions

1. Add all of the above ingredients to your Instant Pot.
2. Secure the lid. Choose "Manual" mode and High pressure; cook for 1 minute. Once cooking is complete, use a quick pressure release; carefully remove the lid.
3. Let cool completely.

Storing

- Spoon your dip into airtight containers; keep in your refrigerator for up to 4 to 7 days.
- For freezing, place your dip in airtight containers or heavy-duty freezer bags. It will maintain the best quality for about 3 to 4 months. Defrost in the refrigerator. Enjoy!

76. Dad's Cocktail Meatballs

Servings 6

**Ready in about
15 minutes**

**NUTRITIONAL
INFORMATION
(Per Serving)**

384 - Calories
22.2g - Fat
5.1g - Carbs
38.4g - Protein
3.6g - Sugars

Ingredients

- 1/2 pound ground pork
- 1 pound ground beef
- 1/2 cup Romano cheese, grated
- 1/2 cup pork rinds, crushed
- 1 egg, beaten
- Coarse sea salt and ground black pepper, to taste
- 1 teaspoon granulated garlic
- 1/2 teaspoon cayenne pepper
- 1/2 teaspoon dried basil
- 1/4 cup milk, lukewarm
- 1 ½ cups BBQ sauce

Directions

1. Thoroughly combine the ground meat, cheese, pork rinds, egg, salt, black pepper, garlic, cayenne pepper, basil, and milk in the mixing bowl.
2. Then, roll the mixture into 20 meatballs.
3. Pour the BBQ sauce into your Instant Pot. Now, add the meatballs and secure the lid.
4. Choose "Manual" mode and High pressure; cook for 8 minutes. Once cooking is complete, use a quick pressure release; carefully remove the lid.
5. Let cool completely.

Storing

- Place the meatballs in airtight containers or Ziploc bags; keep in your refrigerator for up to 3 to 4 days.
- Freeze the meatballs in airtight containers or heavy-duty freezer bags. Freeze up to 3 to 4 months. To defrost, slowly reheat in a saucepan. Bon appétit!

77. Party Chicken Drumettes

Servings 8

Ready in about
15 minutes

NUTRITIONAL
INFORMATION
(Per Serving)

237 - Calories
20.6g - Fat
3.1g - Carbs
10.2g - Protein
1.8g - Sugars

Ingredients

- 2 pounds chicken drumettes
- 1 stick butter
- 1 tablespoon coconut aminos
- Sea salt and ground black pepper, to taste
- 1/2 teaspoon dried dill weed
- 1/2 teaspoon dried basil
- 1 teaspoon hot sauce
- 1 tablespoon fish sauce
- 1/2 cup tomato sauce
- 1/2 cup water

Directions

1. Add all the ingredients to your Instant Pot.
2. Secure the lid. Choose "Poultry" mode and High pressure; cook for 10 minutes. Once cooking is complete, use a natural pressure release; carefully remove the lid.
3. Let cool completely.

Storing

- Place the chicken drumettes in airtight containers or Ziploc bags; keep in your refrigerator for up 3 to 4 days.
- For freezing, place them in airtight containers or heavy-duty freezer bags. Freeze up to 3 months. Once thawed in the refrigerator, heat in the preheated oven at 375 degrees F for 20 to 25 minutes or until heated through. Enjoy!

78. Crave-Worthy Balsamic Baby Carrots

Servings 8

Ready in about 10 minutes

NUTRITIONAL INFORMATION (Per Serving)

94 - Calories
6.1g - Fat
8.9g - Carbs
1.4g - Protein
4.1g - Sugars

Ingredients

- 28 ounces baby carrots
- 1 cup chicken broth
- 1/2 cup water
- 1/2 stick butter
- 2 tablespoons balsamic vinegar
- Coarse sea salt, to taste
- 1/2 teaspoon red pepper flakes, crushed
- 1/2 teaspoon dried dill weed

Directions

1. Simply add all of the above ingredients to your Instant Pot.
2. Secure the lid. Choose "Manual" mode and High pressure; cook for 3 minutes. Once cooking is complete, use a quick pressure release; carefully remove the lid.
3. Let cool completely.

Storing

- Place the baby carrots in airtight containers or Ziploc bags; keep in your refrigerator for up to 3 to 5 days.
- To freeze, arrange the baby carrots on a baking sheet in a single layer; freeze for about 2 hours. Transfer to freezer storage bags. Freeze for up to 3 months. Bon appétit!

79. Chicken Wings Italiano

Servings 12

Ready in about 20 minutes

NUTRITIONAL INFORMATION (Per Serving)

443 - Calories
30.8g - Fat
5.7g - Carbs
33.2g - Protein
3.5g - Sugars

Ingredients

- 4 pounds chicken wings cut into sections
- 1/2 cup butter, melted
- 1 tablespoon Italian seasoning mix
- 1/2 teaspoon onion powder
- 1/2 teaspoon garlic powder
- 1 teaspoon paprika
- 1/2 teaspoon coarse sea salt
- 1/2 teaspoon ground black pepper
- 1 cup Parmigiano-Reggiano cheese, shaved
- 2 eggs, lightly whisked

Directions

1. Add the chicken wings, butter, Italian seasoning mix, onion powder, garlic powder, paprika, salt, and black pepper to your Instant Pot.
2. Secure the lid. Choose "Poultry" mode and High pressure. Cook the chicken wings for 10 minutes. Once cooking is complete, use a natural pressure release; carefully remove the lid.
3. Mix the Parmigiano-Reggiano cheese with the eggs. Spoon this mixture over the wings.
4. Secure the lid. Choose "Manual" mode and High pressure; cook for 4 minutes longer. Once cooking is complete, use a quick pressure release; carefully remove the lid.
5. Let cool completely.

Storing

- Place the chicken wings in airtight containers or Ziploc bags; keep in your refrigerator for up 3 to 4 days.
- For freezing, place the chicken wings in airtight containers or heavy-duty freezer bags. Freeze up to 3 months.
- Once thawed in the refrigerator, heat in the preheated oven at 375 degrees F for 20 to 25 minutes or until heated through. Enjoy!

80. Mexican-Style Broccoli Balls Ole

Servings 8

**Ready in about
25 minutes**

**NUTRITIONAL
INFORMATION
(Per Serving)**

137 - Calories
9.5g - Fat
4.8g - Carbs
8.9g - Protein
1.5g - Sugars

Ingredients

- 1 head broccoli, broken into florets
- 1/2 cup Añejo cheese, shredded
- 1 ½ cups Cotija cheese, crumbled
- 3 ounces Ricotta cheese, cut into small chunks
- 1 teaspoon chili pepper flakes

Directions

1. Add 1 cup of water and a steamer basket to the Instant Pot.
2. Place the broccoli florets in the steamer basket.
3. Secure the lid. Choose "Manual" mode and Low pressure; cook for 5 minutes. Once cooking is complete, use a quick pressure release; carefully remove the lid.
4. Add the broccoli florets along with the remaining ingredients to your food processor. Process until everything is well incorporated.
5. Shape the mixture into balls and place your balls on a parchment-lined baking sheet. Bake in the preheated oven at 390 degrees F for 15 minutes.
6. Let cool completely.

Storing

- Transfer the balls to the airtight containers and place in your refrigerator for up to 3 to 4 days.
- For freezing, place the balls in freezer safe containers and freeze up to 1 month. Defrost in the microwave for a few minutes.

81. Asian-Style Appetizer Ribs

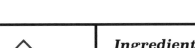

Servings 6

Ready in about 25 minutes

NUTRITIONAL INFORMATION (Per Serving)

331 - Calories
15.8g - Fat
3.1g - Carbs
42.1g - Protein
1.8g - Sugars

Ingredients

- 2 tablespoons sesame oil
- 1 ½ pounds spare ribs
- Salt and ground black pepper, to taste
- 1/2 cup green onions, chopped
- 1 teaspoon ginger-garlic paste
- 1/2 teaspoon red pepper flakes, crushed
- 1/2 teaspoon dries parsley
- 2 tomatoes, crushed
- 1/2 cup chicken stock
- 1 tablespoon tamari sauce
- 2 tablespoons sherry
- 2 tablespoons sesame seeds

Directions

1. Season the spare ribs with salt and black pepper. Press the "Sauté" button and heat the oil. Once hot, brown your spare ribs approximately 3 minutes per side.
2. Add the remaining ingredients, except for sesame seeds, and secure the lid.
3. Choose "Meat/Stew" mode and High pressure; cook for 18 minutes. Once cooking is complete, use a natural pressure release; carefully remove the lid.
4. Sprinkle sesame seed over the top of your ribs.
5. Let cool completely.

Storing

- Divide the ribs into six portions. Place each portion of ribs in an airtight container; keep in your refrigerator for 3 to 5 days.
- For freezing, place the ribs in airtight containers or heavy-duty freezer bags. Freeze up to 4 to 6 months.
- Defrost in the refrigerator. Reheat in your oven at 250 degrees F until heated through. Bon appétit!

82. Zucchini Loaded Meatballs

Servings 8

Ready in about 15 minutes

NUTRITIONAL INFORMATION (Per Serving)

161 - Calories
9.2g - Fat
4.2g - Carbs
14.7g - Protein
2.1g - Sugars

Ingredients

- 1 pound ground turkey
- 1/2 cup Romano cheese, grated
- 1 teaspoon dried basil
- 1/2 teaspoon dried oregano
- 1/2 teaspoon dried dill
- 1 teaspoon dried chives
- 2 tablespoons shallots, chopped
- 1 garlic clove, minced
- 1 egg, beaten
- 1 cup zucchini, grated
- 1 tablespoon olive oil
- 1/2 cup chili sauce
- 1/2 cup broth, preferably homemade

Directions

1. In a mixing bowl, thoroughly combine the ground turkey, grated cheese, basil, oregano, dill, chives, shallots, garlic, egg, and zucchini.
2. Shape the mixture into meatballs.
3. Press the "Sauté" button and heat the oil. Once hot, brown your meatballs for 2 to 3 minutes, turning them occasionally.
4. Add the chili sauce and broth to your Instant Pot. Place the meatballs in the liquid.
5. Secure the lid. Choose "Manual" mode and High pressure; cook for 8 minutes. Once cooking is complete, use a quick pressure release; carefully remove the lid.
6. Let cool completely.

Storing

- Place the meatballs in airtight containers or Ziploc bags; keep in your refrigerator for up to 3 to 4 days.
- Freeze the meatballs in airtight containers or heavy-duty freezer bags. Freeze up to 3 to 4 months. To defrost, slowly reheat in a saucepan. Bon appétit!

83. Party Garlic Prawns

Servings 6

Ingredients

- 2 tablespoons olive oil
- 1 pound prawns, cleaned and deveined
- 2 garlic cloves, minced
- Sea salt and ground black pepper, to taste
- 1 teaspoon cayenne pepper
- 1/2 teaspoon dried dill
- 2 tablespoons fresh lime juice
- 1 cup roasted vegetable broth, preferably homemade

Ready in about 10 minutes

Directions

1. Press the "Sauté" button and heat the olive oil. Once hot, cook your prawns for 2 to 3 minutes.
2. Add the garlic and cook an additional 40 seconds.
3. Stir in the remaining ingredients.
4. Secure the lid. Choose "Manual" mode and Low pressure; cook for 2 minutes. Once cooking is complete, use a quick pressure release; carefully remove the lid.
5. Let cool completely.

NUTRITIONAL INFORMATION (Per Serving)

122 - Calories
5.8g - Fat
2.7g - Carbs
14.2g - Protein
0.5g - Sugars

Storing

- Place the prawns in airtight containers or Ziploc bags; keep in your refrigerator for up 3 to 4 days.
- For freezing, arrange the prawns in a single layer on a baking tray; place in the freezer for about 15 minutes, or until it begins to harden.
- Transfer the frozen shrimp to heavy-duty freezer bags. Freeze up to 3 months. Defrost in your refrigerator. Enjoy!

84. Game Day Sausage Dip

Servings 12

Ready in about 45 minutes

NUTRITIONAL INFORMATION (Per Serving)

251 - Calories
18.3g - Fat
5.8g - Carbs
14.5g - Protein
5.3g - Sugars

Ingredients

- 1 tablespoon ghee
- 3/4 pound spicy breakfast sausage, casings removed and crumbled
- 16 ounces Velveeta cheese
- 8 ounces Cotija cheese shredded
- 2 (10-ounce) cans diced tomatoes with green chilies
- 1 cup chicken broth
- 1 package taco seasoning

Directions

1. Press the "Sauté" button and melt the ghee. Once hot, cook the sausage until it is no longer pink.
2. Add the remaining ingredients.
3. Secure the lid. Choose "Slow Cook" mode and Low pressure; cook for 40 minutes. Once cooking is complete, use a quick pressure release; carefully remove the lid.
4. Let cool completely.

Storing

- Spoon your dip into airtight containers; keep in your refrigerator for up to 4 to 6 days.
- For freezing, place your dip in airtight containers or heavy-duty freezer bags. It will maintain the best quality for about 3 months. Defrost in the refrigerator. Enjoy!

85. Two-Cheese and Caramelized Onion Dip

Servings 12

**Ready in about
15 minutes**

**NUTRITIONAL
INFORMATION
(Per Serving)**

148 - Calories
10g - Fat
5.4g - Carbs
7.5g - Protein
4.1g - Sugars

Ingredients

- 3 tablespoons butter
- 2 pounds white onions, chopped
- Sea salt and freshly ground black pepper, to taste
- 1/4 teaspoon dill
- 1 tablespoon coconut aminos
- 1 cup broth, preferably homemade
- 10 ounces Ricotta cheese
- 6 ounces Swiss cheese

Directions

1. Press the "Sauté" button and melt the butter. Once hot, cook the onions until they are caramelized.
2. Add the salt, pepper, dill, coconut aminos, and broth.
3. Secure the lid. Choose "Manual" mode and High pressure; cook for 10 minutes. Once cooking is complete, use a natural pressure release; carefully remove the lid.
4. Fold in the cheese and stir until everything is well combined. Let cool completely.

Storing

- Spoon your dip into airtight containers; keep in your refrigerator for up to 4 to 6 days.
- For freezing, place your dip in airtight containers or heavy-duty freezer bags. It will maintain the best quality for about 3 months. Defrost in the refrigerator. Enjoy!

86. Umami Party Chicken Wings

Servings 6

Ready in about 15 minutes

Ingredients

- 2 teaspoons butter, melted
- 1 ½ pounds chicken wings
- 1/2 cup chicken broth
- 1/2 cup barbecue sauce
- 1 tablespoon fish sauce
- 1/4 cup rice vinegar
- 1 teaspoon grated fresh ginger
- Sea salt ground black pepper, to your liking
- 1/2 teaspoon cumin
- 1/2 teaspoon caraway seeds
- 1/2 teaspoon celery seeds
- 1/2 teaspoon garlic powder
- 1/2 teaspoon red pepper, crushed
- 2 tablespoons Thai basil

Directions

1. Add the butter, chicken wings, broth, barbecue sauce, fish sauce, vinegar, ginger, and spices to your Instant Pot.
2. Secure the lid. Choose "Poultry" mode and High pressure. Cook the chicken wings for 10 minutes. Once cooking is complete, use a natural pressure release; carefully remove the lid.
3. Garnish with Thai basil. Let cool completely.

Storing

- Place the chicken wings in airtight containers or Ziploc bags; keep in your refrigerator for up 3 to 4 days.
- For freezing, place the chicken wings in airtight containers or heavy-duty freezer bags. Freeze up to 3 months.
- Once thawed in the refrigerator, heat in the preheated oven at 375 degrees F for 20 to 25 minutes or until heated through. Enjoy!

NUTRITIONAL INFORMATION (Per Serving)

200 - Calories
5.5g - Fat
6.8g - Carbs
25.6g - Protein
4g - Sugars

87. Bok Choy Boats with Shrimp Salad

Servings 8

Ready in about
10 minutes

NUTRITIONAL
INFORMATION
(Per Serving)

124 - Calories
10.6g - Fat
3.1g - Carbs
4.7g - Protein
1.8g - Sugars

Ingredients

- 26 shrimp, cleaned and deveined
- 2 tablespoons fresh lemon juice
- 1 cup of water
- Sea salt and ground black pepper, to taste
- 2 tomatoes, diced
- 4 ounces feta cheese, crumbled
- 1/3 cup olives, pitted and sliced
- 4 tablespoons olive oil
- 2 tablespoons apple cider vinegar
- 8 Bok choy leaves
- 2 tablespoons fresh basil leaves, snipped
- 2 tablespoons fresh mint leaves, chopped

Directions

1. Toss the shrimp and fresh lemon juice in your Instant Pot. Add 1 cup of water.
2. Secure the lid. Choose "Manual" mode and Low pressure; cook for 2 minutes. Once cooking is complete, use a quick pressure release; carefully remove the lid.
3. Season the shrimp with sea salt and ground black pepper, and allow them to cool completely. Toss the shrimp with tomatoes, feta cheese, olives, olive oil, and vinegar.
4. Mound the salad onto each Bok choy leaf and arrange them on a serving platter. Top with basil and mint leaves. Let cool completely.

Storing

- Place the Bok Choy boats in airtight containers; it will last for 3 to 4 days in the refrigerator.
- For freezing, place the Bok Choy boats in airtight containers or heavy-duty freezer bags. Freeze up to 3 months. Defrost in the microwave or refrigerator. Bon appétit!

DESSERTS

88. Fabulous Blackberry Brownies

Servings 8

**Ready in about
30 minutes**

**NUTRITIONAL
INFORMATION
(Per Serving)**

151 - Calories
13.6g - Fat
5.7g - Carbs
4.1g - Protein
1.1g - Sugars

Ingredients

- 4 eggs
- 1 ¼ cups coconut cream
- 1 teaspoon Stevia liquid concentrate
- 1/3 cup cocoa powder, unsweetened
- 1/2 teaspoon grated nutmeg
- 1/2 teaspoon cinnamon powder
- 1 teaspoon espresso coffee
- 1 teaspoon pure almond extract
- 1 teaspoon pure vanilla extract
- 1 teaspoon baking powder
- A pinch of kosher salt
- 1 cup blackberries, fresh or frozen (thawed)

Directions

1. Start by adding 1 ½ cups of water and a metal rack to your Instant Pot. Now, spritz a baking pan with a nonstick cooking spray.
2. Now, mix the eggs, coconut cream, Stevia, cocoa powder, nutmeg, cinnamon, coffee, pure almond extract vanilla, baking powder, and salt with an electric mixer.
3. Crush the blackberries with a fork. After that, fold in your blackberries into the prepared mixture.
4. Pour the batter into the prepared pan.
5. Secure the lid. Choose "Bean/Chili" mode and High pressure; cook for 25 minutes. Once cooking is complete, use a natural pressure release; carefully remove the lid.
6. Let cool completely.

Storing

- Place your brownies in airtight containers; keep in the refrigerator for 3 to 4 days.
- For freezing, wrap the brownies tightly with aluminum foil or plastic freezer wrap; freeze up to 4 to 6 months. Defrost in your microwave for a couple of minutes. Enjoy!

89. Mixed Berry Mini Cheesecakes

Servings 6

Ready in about 25 minutes

NUTRITIONAL INFORMATION (Per Serving)

232 - Calories
22.1g - Fat
4.8g - Carbs
5.7g - Protein
1.9g - Sugars

Ingredients

- 1/4 cup sesame seed flour
- 1/4 cup hazelnut flour
- 1/2 cup coconut flour
- 1 ½ teaspoons baking powder
- A pinch of kosher salt
- A pinch of freshly grated nutmeg
- 1/2 teaspoon ground star anise
- 1/2 teaspoon ground cinnamon
- 1/2 stick butter
- 1 cup Swerve
- 2 eggs, beaten
- 1/2 cup cream cheese
- 1/3 cup fresh mixed berries
- 1/2 vanilla paste

Directions

1. Start by adding 1 ½ cups of water and a rack to your Instant Pot.
2. In a mixing dish, thoroughly combine all of the above ingredients. Divide the batter between lightly greased ramekins. Cover with a piece of foil.
3. Place the ramekins on the rack.
4. Secure the lid. Choose "Manual" mode and High pressure; cook for 20 minutes. Once cooking is complete, use a natural pressure release; carefully remove the lid.

Storing

- Place the mini cheesecakes in airtight containers and refrigerate for a week.
- To freeze, place the mini cheesecakes on a baking tray and freeze for 2 hours. Now, place them in airtight containers. They can be frozen for 2 to 3 months. Bon appétit!

90. Romantic Rosewater Dessert Porridge

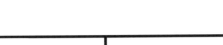

Servings 2

Ready in about 10 minutes

NUTRITIONAL INFORMATION (Per Serving)

363 - Calories
36.4g - Fat
7.1g - Carbs
4.9g - Protein
4.8g - Sugars

Ingredients

- 1/2 cup coconut shreds
- 1 tablespoon sunflower seeds
- 2 tablespoons flax seeds
- 2 cardamom pods, crushed slightly
- 1 teaspoon ground cinnamon
- 1 teaspoon Stevia powdered extract
- 1 teaspoon rosewater
- 1/2 cup water
- 1 cup coconut milk

Directions

1. Add all the ingredients to the Instant Pot.
2. Secure the lid. Choose "Manual" mode and High pressure; cook for 5 minutes. Once cooking is complete, use a quick pressure release; carefully remove the lid.
3. Let cool completely.

Storing

- Divide the porridge into two portions; store each portion in an airtight container. Keep in the refrigerator for up to 5 days.
- To freeze, place each portion in an airtight container; freeze for up to 3 months. Reheat the porridge in a microwave, stirring and adding some extra liquid if necessary. Bon appétit!

91. Grandma's Orange Cheesecake

Servings 10

Ready in about 35 minutes + chilling time

NUTRITIONAL INFORMATION (Per Serving)

188 - Calories
17.2g - Fat
4.5g - Carbs
5.5g - Protein
1.3g - Sugars

Ingredients

- **Crust:**
- 1/2 cup almond flour
- 1/2 cup coconut flour
- 1 ½ tablespoons powdered erythritol
- 1/4 teaspoon kosher salt
- 3 tablespoons butter, melted

- **Filling:**
- 8 ounces sour cream, at room temperature
- 8 ounces cream cheese, at room temperature
- 1/2 cup powdered erythritol
- 3 tablespoons orange juice
- 1/2 teaspoon ginger powder
- 1 teaspoon vanilla extract
- 3 eggs, at room temperature

Directions

1. Line a round baking pan with a piece of parchment paper.
2. In a mixing bowl, thoroughly combine all the crust ingredients in the order listed above.
3. Press the crust mixture into the bottom of the pan.
4. Then, make the filling by mixing the sour cream and cream cheese until uniform and smooth; add the remaining ingredients and continue to beat until everything is well combined.
5. Pour the cream cheese mixture over the crust. Cover with aluminum foil, making a foil sling.
6. Place 1 ½ cups of water and a metal trivet in your Instant Pot. Then, place the pan on the metal rack.
7. Secure the lid. Choose "Manual" mode and High pressure; cook for 30 minutes. Once cooking is complete, use a natural pressure release; carefully remove the lid.
8. Allow your cheesecake to cool completely.

Storing

- Refrigerate your cheesecake covered loosely with plastic wrap. Keep in your refrigerator for up to 7 days.
- To freeze, wrap the cheesecake tightly with foil or place in heavy-duty freezer bag; freeze for about 2 to 3 months. Bon appétit!

92. Coconut and Raspberry Cupcakes

Servings 6

Ready in about
35 minutes

NUTRITIONAL
INFORMATION
(Per Serving)

403 - Calories
42.1g - Fat
4.1g - Carbs
4.2g - Protein
2.1g - Sugars

Ingredients

- **Cupcakes:**
- 1/2 cup coconut flour
- 1/2 cup almond flour
- 1/2 teaspoon baking soda
- 1 teaspoon baking powder
- A pinch of salt
- A pinch of grated nutmeg
- 1 teaspoon ginger powder
- 1 stick butter, at room temperature
- 1/2 cup Swerve
- 3 eggs, beaten
- 1/2 teaspoon pure coconut extract
- 1/2 teaspoon pure vanilla extract
- 1/2 cup double cream

- **Frosting:**
- 1 stick butter, at room temperature
- 1/2 cup Swerve
- 1 teaspoon pure vanilla extract
- 1/2 teaspoon coconut extract
- 6 tablespoons coconut, shredded
- 3 tablespoons raspberry, puréed
- 6 frozen raspberries

Directions

1. Start by adding 1 ½ cups of water and a rack to your Instant Pot.
2. In a mixing dish, thoroughly combine the cupcake ingredients. Divide the batter between silicone cupcake liners. Cover with a piece of foil.
3. Place the cupcakes on the rack.
4. Secure the lid. Choose "Manual" mode and High pressure; cook for 25 minutes. Once cooking is complete, use a natural pressure release; carefully remove the lid.
5. In the meantime, thoroughly combine the frosting ingredients. Put this mixture into a piping bag and top your cupcakes.
6. Let cool completely.

Storing

- Place the cupcakes in airtight containers or cover with foil or plastic wrap to prevent drying out; your cupcakes will last for about 1 to 2 days at room temperature.
- Place your cupcakes in the airtight containers or Ziploc bags; keep in the refrigerator for a week.
- For freezing, wrap the cupcakes tightly with aluminum foil or plastic freezer wrap, or place in heavy-duty freezer bag; freeze up to 4 to 6 months. Defrost in your microwave for a couple of minutes.

93. Vanilla Rum Flan

Servings 6

Ready in about 15 minutes

NUTRITIONAL INFORMATION (Per Serving)

263 - Calories
21.2g - Fat
3.2g - Carbs
10.5g - Protein
2.8g - Sugars

Ingredients

- 6 eggs
- 1 cup Swerve
- 1 ½ cups double cream
- 1/2 cup water
- 3 tablespoons dark rum
- A pinch of salt
- A pinch of freshly grated nutmeg
- 1/4 teaspoon ground cinnamon
- 1 teaspoon vanilla extract

Directions

1. Start by adding 1 ½ cups of water and a metal rack to your Instant Pot.
2. In a mixing bowl, thoroughly combine the eggs and Swerve. Add the double cream, water, rum, salt, nutmeg, cinnamon, and vanilla extract.
3. Pour the mixture into a baking dish. Lower the dish onto the rack.
4. Secure the lid. Choose "Manual" mode and High pressure; cook for 10 minutes. Once cooking is complete, use a natural pressure release; carefully remove the lid.
5. Allow it to cool about 4 hours.

Storing

- Divide the mixture among six airtight containers; it can be stored in the refrigerator up to 3 days.
- Slide the flan into pieces; transfer them to a heavy-duty freezer bag. Store in your freezer up to 1 month. Defrost in the refrigerator. Bon appétit!

94. Blueberry Dessert Porridge

Servings 4

Ready in about 10 minutes

NUTRITIONAL INFORMATION (Per Serving)

219 - Calories
18.2g - Fat
7.2g - Carbs
5.6g - Protein
4.9g - Sugars

Ingredients

- 6 tablespoons golden flax meal
- 6 tablespoons coconut flour
- 2 cups water
- 1/4 teaspoon freshly grated nutmeg
- 1/4 teaspoon Himalayan salt
- 3 egg, whisked
- 1/2 stick butter, softened
- 4 tablespoons double cream
- 4 tablespoons monk fruit powder
- 1 cup blueberries

Directions

1. Add all the ingredients to the Instant Pot.
2. Secure the lid. Choose "Manual" mode and High pressure; cook for 5 minutes. Once cooking is complete, use a quick pressure release; carefully remove the lid.
3. Let cool completely.

Storing

- Divide the porridge into four portions; store each portion in an airtight container. Keep in the refrigerator for up to 5 days.
- To freeze, place each portion in an airtight container; freeze for up to 3 months. Reheat the porridge in a microwave, stirring and adding some extra liquid if necessary. Bon appétit!

95. Chocolate and Hazelnut Birthday Cake

Servings 8

Ready in about 35 minutes + chilling time

NUTRITIONAL
INFORMATION
(Per Serving)

230 - Calories
18.8g - Fat
6.8g - Carbs
8.9g - Protein
1.4g - Sugars

Ingredients

- **Batter:**
- 1 cup hazelnut flour
- 2 tablespoons arrowroot starch
- 1/2 cup cocoa powder
- 1 ¼ teaspoons baking powder
- 1/4 teaspoon kosher salt
- 1/4 teaspoon freshly grated nutmeg
- 6 eggs, whisked
- 8 tablespoons coconut oil, melted
- 1 teaspoon pure vanilla extract
- 1/2 teaspoon pure hazelnut extract
- 2/3 cup Swerve
- 1/3 cup full-fat milk

- **Hazelnut Ganache:**
- 1/2 cup heavy cream
- 5 ounces dark chocolate, sugar-free
- 2 tablespoons coconut oil

Directions

1. Start by adding 1 ½ cups of water and a metal rack to your Instant Pot. Now, lightly grease a baking pan with a nonstick cooking spray.
2. In a mixing bowl, thoroughly combine dry ingredients for the batter. In another bowl, mix wet ingredients for the batter.
3. Add the wet mixture to the dry mixture; mix to combine well. Pour the mixture into the prepared baking pan.
4. Secure the lid. Choose "Bean/Chili" mode and High pressure; cook for 30 minutes. Once cooking is complete, use a natural pressure release; carefully remove the lid.
5. Now, place the cake pan on a wire rack until it is cool to the touch. Allow it to cool completely before frosting.
6. Meanwhile, make your ganache. In a medium pan, bring the heavy cream to a boil. Turn the heat off as soon as you see the bubbles.
7. Add the chocolate and coconut oil and whisk to combine well. Frost the cake and let it cool completely.

Storing

- Cover loosely with aluminum foil or plastic wrap and refrigerate for a week.
- To freeze, place the cake on a baking pan and freeze for 2 hours; then, place in a heavy-duty freezer bag. It will maintain the best quality for about 4 to 6 months. Enjoy!

96. Fudge with Nuts and Neufchatel

Servings 6

Ready in about 10 minutes + chilling time

NUTRITIONAL INFORMATION (Per Serving)

404 - Calories
39.5g - Fat
6.1g - Carbs
8.7g - Protein
3.2g - Sugars

Ingredients

- 10 ounces Neufchâtel cheese, room temperature
- 2 sticks butter
- 3/4 cup hazelnut butter
- 1/2 teaspoon vanilla extract
- 1/2 teaspoon star anise, ground
- 1/2 cup almond flour
- 1 ½ teaspoons stevia powder

Directions

1. Place the cheese, butter, and hazelnut butter in your Instant Pot.
2. Press the "Sauté" button and let it simmer until thoroughly heated.
3. Stir in the other ingredients and continue to stir until everything is well incorporated.
4. Now, spoon the mixture into a square cookie sheet lined with a piece of foil. Transfer to your refrigerator for 2 to 3 hours.

Storing

- Refrigerate your fudge covered loosely with plastic wrap. Keep in your refrigerator for up to 7 days.
- To freeze, wrap your fudge tightly with foil or place in heavy-duty freezer bag; freeze for about 2 to 3 months. Bon appétit!

97. Peanut Butter and Chocolate Mousse

Servings 4

Ready in about 10 minutes

NUTRITIONAL INFORMATION (Per Serving)

372 - Calories
34.5g - Fat
6.7g - Carbs
8.4g - Protein
3.3g - Sugars

Ingredients

• 2 eggs plus 2 egg yolks
• 1 teaspoon liquid Stevia
• 1/4 cup creamy peanut butter
• 1/4 cup cocoa powder
• 1 ½ cups whipping cream
• 1 teaspoon pure vanilla extract
• 1/2 teaspoon pure almond extract
• A pinch of salt
• A pinch of grated nutmeg
• 2 ounces chocolate chips, sugar-free

Directions

1. Whisk the eggs in a bowl. Then, in a saucepan over a moderate heat, cook the Stevia, peanut butter, and cocoa powder. Mix until everything is well incorporated and heated through.
2. Then, mix in the cream, vanilla extract, almond extract, salt, and grated nutmeg.
3. Gradually add the cream mixture to the bowl with the eggs; whisk to combine well. Divide the mixture among four ramekins.
4. Add 1 ½ cups of water and a metal rack to your Instant Pot. Place the ramekins on the rack.
5. Secure the lid. Choose "Manual" mode and High pressure; cook for 8 minutes. Once cooking is complete, use a quick pressure release; carefully remove the lid.
6. Add the chocolate chips to the top. Let cool completely.

Storing

• Divide the chocolate mousse between four airtight containers; keep in the refrigerator for 3 to 4 days.
• For freezing, divide the chocolate mousse between four Ziploc bags and freeze up to 4 to 5 months. Defrost in your microwave for a couple of minutes. Enjoy!

98. Espresso Molten Cake

Servings 6

**Ready in about
10 minutes**

**NUTRITIONAL
INFORMATION
(Per Serving)**

152 - Calories
12.1g - Fat
5.9g - Carbs
7.3g - Protein
1.6g - Sugars

Ingredients

- 1/2 cup cocoa powder, unsweetened
- 1 teaspoon liquid Stevia
- 1/2 teaspoon baking soda
- 1/2 teaspoon baking powder
- 1/8 teaspoon sea salt
- 2 teaspoons espresso powder
- 2 eggs
- 1/2 cup double cream
- 1/4 teaspoon cinnamon powder
- 1/4 teaspoon grated nutmeg
- 1/2 teaspoon vanilla extract

Directions

1. Start by adding 1 ½ cups of water and a metal rack to your Instant Pot. Now, spritz a heatproof bowl with a nonstick cooking spray.
2. Now, whip all the ingredients with an electric mixer.
3. Secure the lid. Choose "Manual" mode and High pressure; cook for 6 minutes. Once cooking is complete, use a natural pressure release; carefully remove the lid.
4. Invert your cake onto the serving platter. Let cool completely.

Storing

- Cover your cake with foil or plastic wrap to prevent drying out; it will last for about 1 to 2 days at room temperature.
- Cover your cake loosely with aluminum foil or plastic wrap and refrigerate for 7 days.
- To freeze, wrap your cake tightly with aluminum foil or plastic freezer wrap, or place in heavy-duty freezer bag; freeze for about 4 to 6 months. Enjoy!

99. Brownie Squares with Blackberry-Goat Cheese Swirl

Servings 8

**Ready in about
30 minutes**

**NUTRITIONAL
INFORMATION
(Per Serving)**

309 - Calories
27.6g - Fat
6.4g - Carbs
10.8g - Protein
2.1g - Sugars

Ingredients

- **Brownies:**
- 5 tablespoons coconut oil, melted
- 1 cup Swerve
- 1/4 cup cocoa powder, unsweetened
- 3 teaspoons water
- 1/2 teaspoon vanilla extract
- 3 eggs, beaten
- 1/4 cup golden flax meal
- 3/4 cup almond flour
- 1/2 teaspoon baking soda
- 1/2 teaspoon baking powder
- A pinch of salt
- A pinch of grated nutmeg
- 1/4 cup chocolate chunks, sugar-free

- **Blackberry Goat Cheese Swirl:**
- 2 tablespoons unsalted butter, softened
- 4 ounces goat cheese, softened
- 2 ounces cream cheese, softened
- 1 cup blackberries, fresh or frozen (thawed)
- 1 tablespoon Swerve
- 1/2 teaspoon almond extract
- A pinch of salt

Directions

1. Start by adding 1 ½ cups of water and a metal rack to your Instant Pot. Now, spritz a square cake pan with a nonstick cooking spray.
2. Mix the coconut oil with the Swerve, cocoa powder, water, and vanilla until well combined. Mix in the eggs, flour, baking soda, baking powder, salt, and nutmeg.
3. Mix until smooth and creamy. Add the chocolate and mix one more time. Add the batter to the prepared pan.
4. Secure the lid. Choose "Manual" mode and High pressure; cook for 25 minutes. Once cooking is complete, use a quick pressure release; carefully remove the lid.
5. Invert your brownie onto a platter. Allow it to cool to room temperature.
6. Meanwhile, make the blackberry-goat cheese swirl. Beat the butter and cheese with an electric mixer; add the blackberries, Swerve, almond extract and salt and continue to beat until light and fluffy.
7. Drop this mixture on top of your brownie in spoonfuls; then swirl it with a knife. Let cool completely.

Storing

- Place your brownies in airtight containers; keep in the refrigerator for 3 to 4 days.
- For freezing, wrap the brownies tightly with aluminum foil or plastic freezer wrap; freeze up to 4 to 6 months. Defrost in your microwave for a couple of minutes. Enjoy!

100. Coconut and Chocolate Fudge

Servings 6

Ready in about 10 minutes + chilling time

NUTRITIONAL INFORMATION (Per Serving)

189 - Calories
19.8g - Fat
5.8g - Carbs
2.1g - Protein
1.6g - Sugars

Ingredients

- 1/2 cup melted coconut oil
- 1/2 cup coconut milk
- 1/2 cup coconut flour
- 1/2 cup cocoa powder
- 1/2 cup Swerve
- 1/4 teaspoon ground cinnamon
- 1/4 teaspoon ground cloves
- 1 teaspoon vanilla paste
- 1 teaspoon coconut extract
- A pinch sea salt
- A pinch of grated nutmeg

Directions

1. Place the coconut oil, milk, flour, cocoa powder, and Swerve in the Instant Pot.
2. Add the remaining ingredients and mix until everything is well incorporated.
3. Press the "Sauté" button and let it simmer stir until thoroughly heated.
4. Now, spoon the mixture into a baking sheet lined with a piece of foil. Transfer to your refrigerator for 2 to 3 hours.

Storing

- Refrigerate the chocolate fudge covered loosely with plastic wrap. Keep in your refrigerator for up to 7 days.
- To freeze, wrap the chocolate fudge tightly with foil or place in heavy-duty freezer bag; freeze for about 2 to 3 months. Bon appétit!

Made in the USA
San Bernardino, CA
10 December 2018